ISBN13: 978-1-64456-204-8
Library of Congress Control Number: 2020947100

INDIES UNITED PUBLISHING HOUSE, LLC
P.O. BOX 3071
QUINCY, IL 62305-3071
www.indiesunited.net

# Recognition and Dedication

First off, I would like to thank God, who gave me the gift to transpose words into making "based on" or "inspired by" true events, for the world to read and be delighted by. My writing is designed to enlighten, inspire and motivate YOU! No one said life would be easy, right? At times it can be very difficult. It only seems to get tougher with each passing day. In these trying times stay strong, have faith, and keep pushing forward! "Thank You" for supporting me! May God bless you in this thing we call life!

Special thanks and dedication to Carl Thompson for allowing me to share parts of his life and giving me the opportunity to portray him as a character in this book.

Special thanks to the fam bam who kept me grounded during this project! Thanks for being my rock, and for always being in my corner. Love you guys to the moon and back!

Thank you to the women whom we call "Grandma." Margaret Gipson and Ola Mae Pratt, two phenomenal women who taught my parents good values and morals which are instilled in me, too. I love you! (R.I.H. Grandmas). <3

Thank you to my cousin Randy Vinson for assisting with the football plays. I would have been so lost without you and that is real talk! <3

A special thanks to the late artist Prince. I have always been a huge fan of Prince. I am fascinated because of his ability as an innovator, musical genius, and a brilliant storyteller. He left behind a wonderful legacy for us to cherish for eternity. The chapter "They Interracially Meet" is a real outcome with a twist of fiction I dedicate to the purple majesty himself. I am so honored to have done so. "They Interracially Meet" is composed of Prince's song titles. It has been a pleasure! Thank You Mr. Prince Rogers Nelson for being an inspiration to me, sharing your creative talent, and the wonderful music you blessed the world. We will be rocking to your music to the end of all time. (R.I.H Prince) <3

A big thank you to Aaron Gallagher editor for having my back with this project.

Britt Wynn, best agent ever.

Thank you to Barbara O'Callaghan, Drill Team and Auxiliaries Director, and Coach Vollnogle (RIP) for making Carson High Champions during the 80's. Thanks for the great times!

I am gracious to my many English teachers. Special thanks to one in particular, Mrs. McMurray who made me aware of my gift. Look at me now! Without you all how would I have done it?

Again, a big thank you to Barbara Watters and Mister (RIH) for helping me find me! <3

Last but not least, Mr. Pepper. Pepper, you more than just a dog, my little best buddy for seventeen years. We explored the world with lots of road trips, and had so much fun together. When it was time for you to transcend it crushed me to pieces. I understand we are borrowed. Rest in heaven, little buddy! <3

Shout out to the storytellers. Whether you get your point across through speaking, books or music. One love!!! <3

# FOOTBALL SUPERSTAR

## Inspired by Real Events

## YETTA YVETTE

INDIES UNITED PUBLISHING HOUSE, LLC

You never know how your life is going to turn out...
Especially when the odds are already against you.

# INTRODUCTIONS

# Queenie's World

It was the summer of 1980; my family and I returned from a two weeks' vacation trip to Louisiana. When my father opened the door, the living room was totally vacant. Thieves had stolen our stuff.

"God damn it!" Daddy said as we looked around our bare home, confused. The culprits had taken the dining set, tv console, and the living room furniture. My sister Dee and I hurried to our bedroom, but the outcome was the same.

"Where's my toys?" Dee whimpered.

"Don't cry Dee." I said. I was sad too, but I could not cry. Instead, I hugged Dee tightly. I was the oldest, so I had to be a big girl and show I was a toughie. Over the years my parents worked really hard for what they possessed. Then some lowlife came along and snatched it up. I was terrified, just knowing some creep had been in our bedroom, snooping around and taking our toys. My brand-new roller derby skates and favorite barbie dolls gone. We lived in Compton for eleven months and now it was time to say good riddance.

My mother had a bun in the oven. We noticed she was eating a lot more, but she hadn't the slightest clue, until she took a pregnancy test that night.

"Honey, I can't stand it anymore. I hate it here! I'm about ready to move the hell out of Compton," Mom said, rubbing her stomach. "Congratulations, you're about to be a father again."

Daddy looked surprised. "Baby, really? That's fantastic news, thank you." Dad kissed mom. "I'm going to get us out of here, don't worry."

Dee and I were happy about the news of the new baby, but being kids we were saddened by the loss of our toys. Toys mean the world to children, and we were without ours. We moped around. While daddy made a police report, mom hugged and assured us everything was going to be all right. Daddy hung up the phone. "Okay, that's done," he said.

"Daddy, the bad man took our toys from the closet too, so Dee and I can't play anymore." I said.

"I'm so sorry kiddos. Daddy and mommy will buy you more toys."

"Okay, but where are we going to sleep, our beds are gone too," I said.

"You two can sleep with us tonight and I will replace your beds tomorrow. Okay?"

I nodded. "Okay."

"Okay, girls. Let's get dressed for bed," Mom said. "I have your gowns from the suitcase."

I was so tired from the trip; it was scary not knowing if the criminals would strike again. That summer was the worst ever. Eventually we moved out of Compton and never looked back. Nine and a half months later we were now living in Carson. It was much nicer.

Mom had given birth to my adorable baby sister Janae. It was Halloween and daddy took us trick or treating while mom stayed home nurturing baby Janae. Later that week Dee and I were enrolled in elementary school.

This is where Dee met Tiff and they became good friends. They were both born in October, only one day apart, which was such a coincidence. One day Tiff invited Dee over her house to play dolls. This is when my mother and I met Tiff, Flip, Karter, and Violet. After spending a great deal of time visiting, we became acquainted with the family, and our friendships blossomed. Karter and Flip were some years older than me. They loved to play football.

Sometimes we would go and support them at their games. This is when I noticed Karter was a great football player.

# Factz About #21

Karter Stephens aspired to become an extraordinary football superstar. He was an awesome player, as his statistics proved. I nicknamed him TQ simply because he was just "too quick" with his arm and his feet. In essence, Karter was an exceptional quarterback, and let me tell you why.

Friday night. The cheerleaders are cheering. "We got the B, what? L what? U and E... P. R. I. D. E."

"We got the blue pride!"

"Yeah, yeah!"

"We got the blue pride!"

A fast-talking sports announcer is calling his name numerous times over the loudspeaker.

"Number twenty-one Karter Stephens, throws a thirty-five yards pass to Johnson."

"Stephens heads for an eight-yard touchdown run in the first quarter."

Every game he ever played was recorded and is locked into his memory. It plays back over and over again. Karter still hears the yelling and screaming from the crowd as if it were yesterday. As we sit and reminiscence taking a trip down memory lane, he tells me his major accomplishments included passing 339 yards and two touchdowns and also making rushes for two touchdowns, as the Colts finally broke through.

These were only a few of his accolades during his high school days. Playing against the Banning Pilots was very challenging. The pressure was on, and of course, both teams wanted to win. Karter had friends on the opposing team, too. In 1984, on a Friday night, the Colts won a championship game over the Banning Pilots 33-20. He led his team to many more victories. Karter's future was bright as the sun. Universities such as New Mexico, Arizona, Hawaii, Purdue, and Washington State were begging for him to play for their colleges because he could pass a football like a bullet. As a kid, he always envisioned the screaming fans shouting out his name. Although the odds were against him, he was determined to fight hard for his passion. Karter had a burning desire in his heart for the game. Making it to the finish line wouldn't be easy, however. It takes diligence, preparation and most importantly dedication.

# Humble Beginnings

Karter and Flip fought over Saturday morning cartoons to watch. Their mother Joyce cooked oatmeal for breakfast.

"Cut it out and stop fighting! You both need to learn how to share," she said.

"I want to watch Superman, put it back!" Karter said.

"Maaan, why do we always have to watch what you want to watch?" Flip asked.

"Because I'm the oldest," Karter said with a laugh.

"Mom, that's not fair," Flip said.

"You boys cut it out! I'm so tired of the noise. You're working my nerves. Karter, thirty more minutes and then Flip you can watch what you want to watch. That's how we gonna settle this."

Tiffany, lying in her crib, began to cry. So, Joyce walked over, cuddled her, and gave her a bottle. "I want you to understand family is everything and I don't want you fighting each other. It's okay to fight together over a cause, but never against each other, okay?"

"Okay," Karter and Flip responded.

"I'm tired of watching tv, anyways. I'm about to go play football with my friends," Karter said. Karter walked over to Joyce and gave her a kiss.

"Okay, but you stay close to home, son," Joyce said.

As Karter was leaving, his father unlocked the door and opened it.

"Hey, where are you going?" Ed asked.

"Hey dad, I'm going to play football with my boys."

"Okay, stay close to home and be careful, man."

"Okay, I'm out."

"Hello, everybody," Ed said.

Flip said, "Hey, dad."

"Honey, how was work?"

"Same ole same ole. I'm short on my paycheck by hundred dollars. Shit, and the rent is due this week too," Ed said.

"Yes, it sure is and the light bill, too." Joyce replied. They kissed and hugged each other, wondering how they would pay the household bills. The pressure of life was overwhelming, as well as raising a family.

After finishing playing football with his friends, Karter came home. He opened the door and it was pitched dark. Joyce walked over to the stove to light a candle. "Baby, the electric company turned the lights off, but we'll get it cut back on."

Karter looked shocked and thought to himself, *how am I going to do my homework?*

Growing up in the late seventies, in South Central Los Angeles wasn't easy street. The territory is predominantly African American and Hispanic. There were no handbooks, or classes that taught survival in the hood. If you were soft, your ass got, got! It was "Survival of the fittest" according to Charles Darwin. In order to continue breathing and staying alive in these stomping grounds, you had to exhibit a bluffing tactic... It was called being TOUGH as hell.

Gang violence permeated the atmosphere. Drugs turned the city into a nightmare. Some women would do just about anything for their drug of choice – even selling their precious bodies for as low as five dollars. It was a very devastating time. Everyone had someone in their family hooked on the shit. It destroyed many people and their families. Gangs fought over turfs to sell their drugs. There were two sets, the Bloods, and the Crips. The color red represented the Bloods, and blue represented the Crips. The hood was a hard-knock life. While walking in Los

Angeles on any given day, you would see raggedy houses, giant hood rats, roaches, filthy piss-covered sidewalks and discarded forty-ounce bottles of Old English beer lying in the streets. Old sneaker shoes dangling over electrical wires cables strung across abandoned graffiti-covered buildings, and the acrid scent of gun smoke lingered alongside yellow tape, and chalk outlines.

Living in the ghetto was like living in a jungle. You had to be strong in order to stay alive. The ghetto is populated by the impoverished. The projects; a world where the rich and famous would not (or could not) stand a chance. Karter's mother and father, who were both addicted to heroin, worked hard, trying their very best to provide a better life for their three children. Karter's vicious memories haunted him as he reminisced. His footsteps echoed inside the house. Normally, before he'd opened the door, his mother would greet him with a "Hello son," and a warm smile. On this gruesome day, her body was lying on the floor, cold and still. He felt totally numb as he stared at the horrific sight in front of him. Karter ran over to her, shaking her leg, weeping. "Wake up, Mama! Wake up, Mama! I love you! Please wake up, Mama!"

That time it was only a nightmare and even as he woke up drenched in sweat, the realization that it could be a premonition of what was to come, chilled him to the bone.

Imagine losing your mother to death this way, at the young age of only eleven. The nurturing, the helping you get ready for school, making your lunches, helping you with your homework, being there to encourage you, and giving you love whenever you needed it is completely gone forever. Chaos and turmoil enveloped his family. Several family members blamed his father, and their accusations drove a crushing wedge between them. Karter eventually got the nerve to question his estranged father about it. When he dialed the telephone, thinking of the devastation of his family, his rage only grew stronger.

Karter crumpled up the piece of paper with the telephone number on it and threw it to the ground.

"Hello?" Ed answered.

Karter then went straight for his jugular. "Why did that happen to my mother? You're my father! You were supposed to protect her. How? How could you do that to us?" Karter's voice crackled with anger.

Ed snarled, "You, wait one damn minute! I'm your father, and you're gonna show some damned respect for me!"

Karter laughed. "Really. Respect? For my father, who killed my mother! What kind of man gives drugs to his wife? Someone he loves?"

Ed was speechless. He didn't know how to respond. Karter's words cut like a knife. Ed was consumed with guilt. He hung up without a word.

Karter and Ed became even more distant. Young Karter quickly became a worried, disconsolate kid. He would stare off into space. The phantom of depression lurked anxiously in the shadows of darkness to get him. Visionary nightmares haunt his mind as well as his soul. He finds himself dodging away to the left and creeping away to the right to avoid the demon beast who keeps calling his name. The tone is crisp, and he keeps whispering, "Karter, Karter, Karter!" This evil monster wants to tackle him to the ground and wrestle. He fought extremely hard through it.

Karter, his younger brother Flip, and their sister Tiff went to live with their grandmother, Violet. Living with Violet was not much better. Ghetto life started to influence Karter in the wrong ways. At times, the refrigerator was bare. Karter and Flip would walk down to the corner liquor store. They had no money, so they did what they had to do in order to keep their bellies quiet. Once inside the store, they went berserk.

"Hey, Flip! The honey buns are over here, man."

"Oh, okay! Yeah, boy, I'm getting some Doritos and Now and Later, too. I'll be over there in a minute," Flip said.

The two were so focus on grabbing food they didn't realize trouble had just walked in.

"Fool, where you from? What set you claim?" Two young thugs asked.

Karter was not a fighter. "We don't want any trouble man," he said. Flip, on the other hand, was always down to stir up shit, or turn up for whatever reason. He rushed over to Karter's side.

"We not claiming nothing, just trying to get some munchies, man. What's up, can we do that?" Flip held his hands straight up in the air, as if ready to kick somebody's ass. He didn't show any signs of fear. The two young punks walked closer to Karter and Flip. The Korean store owner broke it up.

"You boys cut it out!" He clapped his hands. "Hurry up and buy, or get out of my store!" Karter and Flip already had their goodies tucked away on them.

On the walk home, the circling of helicopters and police sirens signaled that crime wasn't too far away. A woman screamed, "Stop, stop!" as she was victimized. You could hear the sounds of glass shattering as thieves busted into cars, and stole their radios. All this happened in the broad daylight. It was murderously dangerous living in South Central.

When it came to her family, Violet would not have any nonsense. The children had to be inside the house right before the sun went down and the street lights came on. Violet's voice echoed as she called out their names one by one. "Karter, Flip, and Tiff, get your butts in this house!"

"Flip, Grandma is calling us!" Karter shouted.

"I guess we have to stop playing football, dang!"

"Dang, man!"

"Yeah, I guess we have to go now. Grandma's getting louder."

"Let's go!"

If they had their way, they'd play football all night long with some of the other kids in the neighborhood. It was the happening thing, especially on the weekends.

Karter and Flip had a good brotherly relationship. They were close in age, only three years apart. Karter was older, and calmer. Flip was a little on the wilder side. He didn't take any shit. On any given day or time, he would flip out on someone's ass, especially if he felt it was necessary. He was tough as leather. Growing up in the hood had made him resilient.

Karter grabbed the football from his buddy Jordan. "Okay, fellas, see you guys later, alligators!" Karter and Flip ran towards the house as fast as they could.

Tiffany looked around and stopped playing hopscotch with her girlfriends. She began running at top speed too. Tiff was the baby girl of the bunch. She was feisty, and could be a bit of a spoiled bra, but she loved being their younger sister. Whenever she got into trouble, she was always quick to say, "I'm going to get my big brothers on you!" Suddenly the situation would turn out for the better.

Violet's blaring voice called out their names again. "Karter, Flip, and Tiff!"

"Alright Grandma, Violet, here we come!" they shouted back. Once the children made it inside the house, Violet had words of wisdom for them. "Look here, children. I don't want you to think of granny as the grumpy-ass mean old lady who won't let you play football and hopscotch, okay? I am just trying to protect y'all from harm's way. Do you know how dangerous it is out there in those streets? It is not like how it used to be in the olden days! Damn it, this world is filled with some wicked people! Do you know innocent people are dying every day? Like you and me."

At first Karter, Flip and Tiff were focused on Violet's speech, but due to the commotion going on outside, they were easily distracted. They glanced towards the direction of the window as they heard six gunshots. It sounded like a war outside.

"Get down, children!" Violet said. While lying on the floor terrified, as the police and paramedic rushed to the scene, Violet prayed frantically.

"Lord Jesus protect and watch over us in this scary place we call home. We are stuck here with nowhere else to go because we can't afford to go anywhere else. So please shield us from the gun bullets and the destruction of being prisoners in our own home, because living in the ghetto is not a joke. I am begging and pleading in your son Jesus' name, amen!"

The noise ceased. It seemed the violence had subsided. The children assisted Violet off the floor.

"Look at me, children. Listen, I want you to hear me. Innocent people are dying every day. Like you and me! Always remember this: only the strong survive!"

The boys looked terrified. Tiff's smirk dropped from her face.

"Do you guys hear me?"

With terror in their eyes, the paralyzed children stared at their grandmother. "Yes. We hear you, grandma."

"You may think I am being really strict but you will thank me for it later. I may be a little overprotective and it is only because I love you three kiddos to death. I promised your mother I would always take good care of you and I intend on doing just that!"

With hugs and kisses, they said, "We love you too, granny!"

"Okay, wash up for dinner and then it is off to bed."

Violet had cooked their favorites. When they made it to

the dinner table, their eyes bulged and mouths salivated. Three plates were filled with delicious fried chicken, collard greens, macaroni & cheese, chili beans, sweet yellow cornbread, candied yams, and for dessert some buttery Pillsbury cinnamon rolls. The aroma of the food intensified their hunger.

"Tiff, look! There's a spider crawling on you!" Flip said.

Tiff jumped up out of her chair. She screamed and shook her body. "Where is it, Flip? Where is it?" She started crying. "Get it off me!"

While she spun around, Flip took a piece of fried chicken right off her plate. He motioned to Karter to be quiet. Flip laughed at Tiff.

Violet saw the prank Flip had pulled on Tiff. "I see that shit! Flip, put the chicken back on your sister's plate and stop it!"

"Alright, grandma."

Violet's food was delicious and tasted finger-licking good, just like KFC, and they quickly devoured it. After dinner, the boys and Tiff could barely move. Their bellies were heavy and full.

"How was the food?" Violet asked.

"It was so delicious, granny!" Karter said, while Flip and Tiff just nodded their heads.

As they sat, a rat dashed across the living room floor. Karter leaped up from the table. "Grandma, did you see that shit?"

"Excuse me, young man? What did you just say?"

"Oh, excuse me. I said 'did you see it?'"

Violet cracked up . "Okay, that's much better! Yeah, I seen it. It looks like we have a visitor again."

"Again? Dang!" Flip said. "Grandma, why do we have to live this way? Why?"

Violet look very concerned. Violet always stayed optimistic, and her faith was always strong. "Baby boy, I know. But by the grace of God things will eventually get better for us. God will make a way! You best believe. He will make a way! I promise. Don't you guys worry, okay?"

"Grandma, I know it will get better." Karter said, "because I am going to make it better for us! I am going to get us out of here!"

Karter sounded so determined. He walked over to the cupboard and picked out a mouse trap. Being the oldest, Karter took on the responsibilities of a father's role around the house. "Grandma, I 'll set a trap."

Violet nodded. "Okay, but afterwards it is time for bed."

Flip and Tiff took the dirty dishes to the sink.

Violet had more words of wisdom for them. "Listen, because you are black, just know you are going to have to work like hell. Twice as hard, no matter what, if you want to live a better life! The world does not owe you a damn thing! Always remember! Do you hear me?"

"Yes, ma'am," Flip said.

"I hear you... loud and clear!" Tiff said. She walked over to Violet, and gave her a bear hug and a kiss. "Love you granny!"

Karter and Flip joined them for a group hug.

"Sweet dreams, my babies."

"Good night, grandma! We love you too!"

Once Karter and Flip jumped into their beds, they conversed about their penury lifestyle until falling to sleep. Reality weighed heavy on them both. Flip stared at the ceiling. "Karter, do you think we are ever going to get out of this funky hellhole ghetto?"

"Flip, it's tough to say, but I am going to work damned hard. I got to make it happen! You can bet on it! Do you know how much money's in pro sports?"

"Lots."

"Yeah, man. Millions," Karter said. "I want to be a part of it. The thought of being poor forever pisses me the hell off." Karter was so angry with his life. He rolled over and kicked the wall as hard as he could. Surprisingly, he didn't put a huge hole in it.

Flip raised up from his bed. "Bro, are you okay?"

"Yeah, I'm good. I hate it here!"

Flip wore a disgusted look. "I know man. Me too."

"Flip, we both have to work our asses off so we can get what we want out of life. We have to fight extra hard every day for our dreams, so we can live better. Practice football and constantly study so we can both go to college. We can do it. I know we can!"

"Bro, alright. Time for us to get some shut eye." Flip said.

Karter turned off the light switch. "Good night, Flip."

"Good Night, Karter."

"Love you, man!"

"Love you too, big brother!"

As time passed, the crime in L.A. became more and more outrageous. Innocent bystanders were shot down for no apparent reason. In most cases, it was because he or she was wearing the wrong colors, red or blue. Wearing the wrong colors at the wrong time in the wrong territory often proved deadly. What a crying shame to be caught up in such a travesty. Violet was so terrified; Karter and his siblings could end up unlike so many unfortunate others. Stretched out dead, in a black body bag.

Karter and his family wanted so desperately to escape from the drama and the bullshit. The months quickly passed by. It was November 12, 1977. The Dallas Cowboys was playing the Washington Redskins. Aunt Jackie pointed at the television screen. "Karter, do you want to play football like Tony Dorsett?" she asked.

Karter's eyes lit up like the lights on a Christmas tree and his voice was ecstatic. "Yeeeeesssss! Aunt Jackie, football could be our ticket out of this lifestyle."

"Yes, baby. You can do whatever, if you put your mind to it," she said.

Karter envisioned himself in the NFL, and it felt good to have the support of his family. As time progressed, the stresses of peer pressure became severely devastating. As early as the seventh grade, Karter was propositioned to do drugs, and a lot of times the coercion was at school.

"Hey, TQ! Check this out," Chris said.

Karter strolled over to the fellas. "What y'all smoking?"

"It's weed! Do you want to get high with us?" Anthony asked.

"Nah, man I don't do that shit!" Karter gave the joint back to Anthony. "I heard it kills your brain cells."

"I don't care what it does. I just want to get fucked up," Chris said. They laughed.

"But I don't," Karter interjected, irritated. "I have to keep my mind right, body tight, and clean for football. Man, how could you ask me that shit, anyways? You know I play."

Jordan walked over to the guys. "What's up, Jordan!" Karter said.

"Let's go, man. We don't want to be late for practice."

"Fellas, I have to get to practice. I will catch up with you guys later!" Karter said, and held up a peace sign.

This group was definitely not a good crowd to hang around. Karter left with Jordan, knowing he made the right decision. Junior high and high school were tough, with lots of peer pressure. Because of his mother, Karter was horrified by drugs and never curious about them. So he stayed away from it. His grandmother despised the ghetto, and the effects it had on her grandchildren. Eventually, Violet relocated her family to a peaceful city. They no longer had to live in fear and be on edge. The sky was clean, the air was clean, and it was tranquil in Carson, California.

You could hear the birds chirping. The children could

play outside with their toys, without their parents fearing the worst; bullets ricocheting and hitting their children. Violet was more relaxed here and so were Karter, Flip, and Tiff. Karter was twelve years old, and in a brand-new school. The new school was much different than his previous one. The students' diversity ranged from Caucasian, African, Hispanic, Samoan, and Asian heritage. Unlike the low budget school he had previously attended, where everyone was either black or Hispanic.

Karter's spirit was free, and his mind grew more focused on what his aspirations and football. He played three years of Pop Warner, and he really enjoyed it.

School crushes were few, because his exclusive girlfriend was football. Being devoted only to it and spoiling it to death kept his undivided attention.

After a long day in school, Karter came home. Violet sat on the couch, chewing on some tobacco. He seemed to be in a funk when he sat down next to her. Violet spit out the tobacco in a tin cup. "What's wrong with you? How was your day at school?"

"School was good. I'm just missing my mother a lot."

"Oh son, I know. I miss her greatly too. I know it's never easy. Some days hit harder than others. The grief will always be there, but over time it'll get a little easier. Okay, you hang in there, you hear me?"

"Okay," he replied, sounding as though he was going to cry.

"Come here and give granny a hug." She gripped Karter tightly.

"Thanks, grandma, it still hurts but I'll be alright. I'm going to get started on my homework."

"Okay, I'll be right here, if you need me."

He kissed her on her cheek.

"Oh, by the way, the dryer isn't working again, so in a minute I have to hang some clothes on the line."

"All right," he said.

"Oh, your father called you too."

"A'aight." He went to his room and worked on his homework until it was time to go to bed. When the night fell, Karter felt so abandoned and alone. His mother's death made him feel totally lost and incomplete. Nighttime gave him a chance to reflect on to his past. Whenever he did his pillow would be soaked, wet from his tears. His heart was broken, filled with overwhelming grief. He often questioned God for what his mind could not comprehend. Staring up at the heavenly skies above, he would ask, God, why me? Why can't I have my mother here with me like Jordan and Billy? Why?"

While the other young football players had the love and support of their mothers, Karter did not. He would never ever hear the encouraging words coming from his mother, saying, "Son, I love you! Go out onto the field, and make your mama proud!"

Instead, he had to fantasize about it. Just to hear it once would have mean the world to him. He would have never ever take it for granted, unlike, some of the other kids on the team.

In twelfth grade the pressures magnified. Every eye focused on Karter Stephens, number twenty-one. He wore a powder blue and white jersey, and was the gossip of the school. At practice he steadily prepared himself for his future career. He hadn't chosen to be a role model, but it came with being a football superstar.

One day, out of the blue, Karter received a phone call from his father. When he answered the telephone, he could hear the awkwardness in Ed's trembling voice. "Hello?"

"Hello, son. How are you? I've been thinking a lot lately. I want to apologize for the past, man."

"You can't imagine what it has done to me."

"When your mother died, my heart broke and my world

crumbled."

"I really miss her so much!"

"Damn, I loved that woman. To feel responsible for her death doesn't make me feel good, either. Honestly, I feel like a piece of shit! Every day it is killing me softly, man. I am so sorry!" Ed broke down crying. It was quiet for a few seconds. There had been so much distance with animosity between the two of them. Ed wanted to start fresh and try to repair their broken relationship, but he didn't know what to say, so he just waited for Ed to speak.

"So how's football?"

Football was a topic Karter was always eager to talk about. "It's all good!"

"When is your next game? I would love to stop by and check you out, boy."

At first, Karter was a little reluctant to answer. His heart could not stand any more disappointments, but despite his hesitation, he said, "Ummmm... all right. My next game is this Friday night at eight o'clock. I'm playing against Crenshaw at the Long Beach Veterans Stadium. Look, man, don't say you're coming if you are not going to show up. I don't need any more freaking let-downs from you!"

Ed cleared his throat. "No, son, I will be there. Front and center, you have my word! I promise! C'mon, just give me the information and I will see you then."

"Alright!" While giving his father the address, Karter's heart was blissful. After getting off the telephone, he stared into space. He wondered intensely about the future of his family.

The next day, the bell rung and it was time for football practice. After the roll call, Coach V looked over his clipboard. "Men, we have a game on Friday against Crenshaw High!"

"Yes, sir!" The team shouted.

"Okay, guys I have a great practice lined up for y'all.

First, you're going to start off with some warm up drills. Karter, I want you to focus only on passing. Everyone else'll run laps and practice catching. Men, let's get to work!"

"Okay, Coach V!"

Karter was dead tired, but whenever he stepped out onto the field it always gave him a mighty adrenal rush. The guys formed a huddle.

"On the count of three."

"One, two, three... Carson Colts!"

"Woo!" Karter yelled. He clapped his hands and screamed to the top of his lungs. "I'm ready... let's do this!" He was so pumped up. He had a sense of belonging, and was filled with purpose. He had to prove he was one of the best quarterbacks to ever play. According to the field thermometer, it was a chilly Saturday night in California. The temperature had dropped to the low fifties. It was so freezing cold; he could see the misty frost coming from his breath. The time was getting closer to kick-off. Karter's nerves were bugging, but he anticipated one thing only, and it was winning the football game. Play after play, the opposing team was kicking their asses. Coach V called for a quick timeout so he could discuss some rigorous plays.

"Karter, I need you to do your thing tonight!" Pointing at his clipboard, Coach V directed Karter. "Okay, here's what I want you to do."

Karter looked directly at his coach.

"Karter, Y shallow cross-trail, shake z cross. You got it, man?"

"Yeah, I got it, coach!"

Karter looked around and saw his father making his way to the bleachers. It was the beginning of the third quarter. Although his father had missed half of the football game, Karter could not be angry with him. At least he'd kept his promise and he was making an effort. A Kool-Aid smile transformed Karter's face. The crowd was at the edge of their seats. How were they going to come back from this huge deficit?

The Colts were being defeated in the worst way. Play after play, they were shut down by Crenshaw. Ten minutes were left on the clock, and Gerald Green signaled to the referee for another quick time out. Twenty-two determined players rushed to the sideline. Coach V gave Karter another run-by-run play. It seemed like the game was slipping right between their fingers, and in order to make it to the finals they had to get the win. Coach V came up with a magnificent play, which brought them within range. The score was Crenshaw 20, and the Carson Colts 19. It was at the top of the fourth quarter. The Colts were only one point away from tying the game. Again, twenty-two exhausted players went rushing to the sideline.

Coach V pulled his clipboard. "Fellas, we need some strong defense out there! So, listen up! Vinson, I need you to cover 3 sky. Do you understand me?"

"Yes, sir! Got it, coach!" Vinson said.

"Okay, let's get this game!" The coach made eye contact with Stephens. "On the count of three... one, two, and three!"

"Carson Colts!" the team shouted. This time around the defense was extremely tight. The Colts were able to bury Crenshaw deep of their own short line. Eventually, they took over the lead with a touchdown run by Jerry Gonzales on the ensuing kick out. There were only a few minutes left on the clock. Crenshaw had possession of the ball.

Play after play, the Colts shut them down. It was back in the hands of Karter Stephens, number twenty-one. He scoped and scrambled around the field for an open man. Karter located jersey number forty-five, Jordan Kelly. He was standing near the fifty-yard line. Gripping the football extra tightly, Karter passed it at the speed of a rushing bullet. Jordan was awaiting the pass. The football sped and twirled so rapidly in the air. Kelly caught it, and sprinted off to the endzone.

Touchdown! The band played "Louie, Louie" as Kelly busted out with his signature dance: the cabbage patch and the moonwalk.

"Woo!" Karter screamed. The crowd was absolutely rumbustious and hysterical.

Time for the kick-off. The stadium was as quiet as a mouse. The referee blew the whistle with his arms up in the air. "It's good!" he signaled. The final score was 26 to 20!

After the game, Ed excitedly walked onto the football field, so he could congratulate Karter on his win.

"Congratulations, man! You're good! Where did you get the ability?" With the same offhand comment, Ed praised himself and took credit for his son's talent. Karter just stared at him. Ed started laughing, and said more modestly, "What can I say? I was very athletic in my younger days too, son."

"Thanks," Karter replied. "It's what I love, and it's very important to me. I am passionate, driven, and focused. I've made a lot of sacrifices for the game of football. Because anything worth having there is going to be an expensive price to pay. Plus, you have to fight like hell every day for it... no matter what!"

"You're definitely right, son. I know you have the characteristics to excel, and be the greatest quarterback ever. I wish you nothing but success and the best!" Ed rested his hand on Karter's shoulder. "Son, I am always here for you if you ever need me."

Karter just stared at him in disbelief.

"Do you hear me son? If you ever need anything don't hesitate to let me know." Ed reiterated.

Karter was dumbstruck. He couldn't believe his ears. Karter had only one word to say. "Okay!"

Over the years, he had always had the love and support

of his family. But these exact words coming from his father's mouth meant a lot more to him. His heart yearned for the love of his father, and he so desperately needed it. A father's love is the most important factor in the world. It facilitates in a child's development, and shapes most young boys into becoming strong exceptional men. With time, Karter did learn to forgive his father for their difficult past. Ed's newfound interest was to be able to have a loving father and son relationship. For example, hanging out on the weekends at sports game, enjoying a Budweiser Beer together, fishing, teaching Karter how to shave, and how to work. Exemplifying how to become a man is what Karter wanted, and needed the most from his father.

By the mid-eighties the latest musical fads were hip hop and breakdancing. Break-dancers were pulling out their cardboard, and laying them down on the concrete as floor pads. Showing off his or her vibrant moves and fancy footwork, trying to be like Boogaloo Shrimp or Shabadoo from the movie, "Breakin'."

Karter was fascinated. He loved listening to the music. The sound of Doug E. Fresh scratching, and mixing had become his obsession. There was a knock at the door. "Who is it?" Karter asked.

"It's Flip!" Even though they shared the room, Flip wanted to be respectable. Karter was in deep concentration.

"Come in," Karter said.

"What's up bro?"

Karter instantly stopped the music. "I'm just messing around with this music. What's going on with you?"

"This new chick at school, man! Baby doll is the bomb like boom!" Flip was on cloud nine.

Karter laughed. "She's all that, huh?

"Yes, she's all that and a bag of Lays Sour Cream & Onion Potato Chips." Flip snapped his fingers and laughed. "I think I'm in love with her."

"C'mon, man!" Karter gave him a look. "Don't start getting mushy on me. Do you remember what we talked about?"

Flip looked puzzled. "What? That night... are you serious?"

Karter said, "Flip, we have to stay focused... no matter what!" Karter put his finger up to his head. "Man, stay focused!"

"Alright. This is going to be tough, though." Flip said. "She is fine and she has a fat ass, too."

Karter shook his head. "Little bro, you have to control your hormones. We can have fun, but don't get too serious with the females. Okay?"

"Okay." Flip said.

"I have to get back to my music, man."

"A'aight!" They gave each other some dap. "Peace out!" Flip said.

Karter used music as his escape from the stresses of the outside world. Whenever he was going through an emotional time, he turned to hip hop music for his release. It soothed his soul. He was great at scratching. By doing so, it also made him feel at the peak of his football game. He dealt with the strong force of life as he grew closer to becoming an adult. Karter felt more and more alienated, he had to find himself as a man. As the months on the calendar changed, it brought tougher and tougher times, which financially hit his family hard. Violet did her very best when it came to making ends meet with the allocated funding, she was given welfare to support her grandchildren. But it never seemed to be enough, especially for Karter. High school can become pretty expensive, between nutrition, clothing, school supplies, and his football gear. Although Ed told Karter to never hesitate, he always did. Because of his previous disappointments, his pride always made him feel afraid to call and make a request. Therefore, he would not ask Ed for anything.

When the alarm clock sounded, the sun was out so bright. Karter got dressed for school. He arrived on campus and made his way to class. He sat in his assigned seat, and as soon as he sat down, his stomach rumbled. Karter clenched his belly.

Mrs. Randall wrote a question on the chalkboard. He hoped she wouldn't call his name, and of course she does. "Karter, can you tell me where the adjective is in the sentence, and what does adjective mean?"

Sweating, he cleared his throat. Grrrrrrr... his stomach kept growling. He looked around hoping no one could hear it. When you were hungry, it was difficult trying to stay focused. "Um... red describes the bird, and an adjective is a word or phrase naming an attribute, added to or grammatically related to a noun to modify or describe it."

"That is correct, Karter. Great job!"

"Thank you, Mrs. Randle." After Karter answered the question, he started daydreaming of what he was going to eat for lunch. He fantasized about a fat juicy cheeseburger, French fries, and a Sprite. He couldn't wait to get to the cafeteria. "Sounds good to me," he mumbled to himself.

"Class, your homework assignment tonight is a two-page report on William Shakespeare, and it's due in one week." As the class moaned, the bell rung. Karter stood up. His clothes were a little on the just-getting-by side. He was unable to wear the latest fashions like some of the other kids. Sometimes it caused some ridicule, especially from Garrett. There was always going to be a person in life who was filled with a lot of jealousy. Karter had his adversary, and his name was Garrett. Karter was loved by most of the students at school and hated by one; Garrett. His enemy would do just about anything to embarrass him. Karter the future football superstar walked through the school's campus.

Garrett's evil eyes were watching him. "Hey Karter!" Garrett pointed at his shoes. "What's up with your ugly ass shoes, man? You can't afford no Converse or Nikes? Damn, dude! You look like you had those kicks for a century."

A nearby circle of kids overheard Garrett's insults and laughed.

"I'm not for your bullshit today, Garrett! I'm on my way to practice. Bug off, and leave me the hell alone!" When it was necessary, Karter knew how to clap back. His uncle taught him to use self-defense with his words, instead of using his fist. Fists were only to be used if it was the last alternative. But it was still annoying having to deal with the nonsense on a daily basis. In life, you will always run across haters, and it was evident that Garrett was one. Karter's shoes were worn out and dirty, with cardboard in each of them, to cover up the holes in the soles. Kids could be so darned cruel. He tried not to let the teasing bother him, but it always did, to some degree. Because of his struggles, it made him even more determined, driven, and focused on becoming a quarterback in the NFL. He did not want to have these kinds of worries on his already troubled mind. He often wondered about life and his uncertain future. The questions always floated around in his head. Will I make it? How would it feel to be financially straight, not have to worry about bills being paid, food on the table, and clothes on my back? How would my grandmother feel to not have to live paycheck to paycheck, or rob Peter to pay Paul? How would it really feel to be able to wake up every morning with a carefree state mind?

Karter strongly desired to find out the answers to his questions, even though being rich and famous has another set of problems of its own.

When it came to subjects like algebra, geometry, trigonometry, and calculus, they wrecked his brain. It was a total nightmare for Karter. He strained his cranium to comprehend these subjects. It wasn't easy to concentrate, especially if he was hungry a lot of the time, but he did it. The school days were extremely tough for him, but Karter stayed focused, and kept right along pushing forward to his true love, football.

His future would be based on how well he performed with the football. Karter knew college football would not be easy. The thought always dwelled with him, which meant he had to be the very best at it. Every single game he had to give a hundred and fifty percent, no less. As graduation grew closer, there were so many important decisions to make. He often thought about which college he would attend.

Karter was getting so many acceptance letters traveling through the mail. In fact, he received one letter stating two football scouts were present at his last game against Crenshaw. The recruiter was interested in a sit-down meeting to discuss a scholarship. The pressure increased. Every single college acceptance letter Karter contemplated hard.

"Which school would be the best choice for me and football?" he asked himself. The uncertainty floated around in his head.

Saturday afternoon, Karter and Tiff were playing monopoly. She rolled the dice, and landed on Connecticut Ave.

"Looks like you owe me some dough, sis," Karter said, laughing.

"Ugh, you make me sick. Here." Tiffany handed Karter six hundred dollars.

Karter sang, "Money, money, money!" from the song by the O'Jays.

"Alright already, Karter. Can you help me with my math homework later?" Tiff asked.

"What are you having problems with?"

"Multiplication and division," she said, looking frustrated.

"Of course, I've got you," he said.

The telephone rang. Violet answered.

"Hello?"

"Hello, Madam. I'm Coach Jackson, the head coach here at Arizona State University. How are you?"

"I am well, thank you," Violet answered.

"Great! Can I please speak to Karter Stephens?"

"Yes, sure! One moment, please. Karter, the telephone is for you!" Violet bellowed.

When Karter made it to the telephone, Violet whispered, "It's a recruiter from Arizona State University."

Karter answered the telephone, excited and extremely nervous. His voice shook a little. "Hello, this is Karter."

"Hello Karter, I'm Coach Jackson, one of the top coaches over here at Arizona State University. The reason I'm calling you is because me and two other scouts were at your last game, against Crenshaw. You were simply phenomenal, man!"

"Wow, really? Just doing what I do," Karter said modestly.

Coach Jackson laughed. "I would like you to consider playing for our school. Why don't you think about it, young man? Kick it around in your head. I will get back with you in a week or so for your decision."

Karter was ecstatic. "Alright, sounds great! Thanks, Coach Jackson."

"No problem, Karter. At that time, we'll discuss your scholarship, too. If you agree to accept the offer, Coach Craig will make the visit to your home, okay?" Coach Jackson asked.

"Okay, thank you so much Coach Jackson! I really appreciate it!"

"Okay, good-bye, Karter."

When Karter hung up the telephone, he danced around in a circle, and let out a loud scream. "Woo hoo!"

His grandmother rushed from her bedroom to the living room. "Karter, are you okay? By the sound of your holler it must have been a hell of a conversation."

"Yes, it was good, grandma! Nah, it was better than good, it was awesome! Please sit down, and I will tell you all about it." They sat. "Grandma, the recruiters at my last football game against Crenshaw loved my performance! They're considering me for a full scholarship to Arizona State."

"Really, son? A full scholarship!"

"Yes, grandma! Can you believe it?"

Violent smiled. "That is fantastic! Boy, I know your mother is smiling in heaven. She is so proud of you! We all are! You keep up the good work, and continue to make us proud, okay?"

"Okay, grandma. I made a promise to you. Do you remember?"

Violet gave Karter a knowing look. "Yes, I still remember, son."

"I will always keep my promise. I love you, grandma!"

Violet's eyes got teary as they hugged. "I love you too Karter!" Violet kissed him on his head.

The week flew by and the phone rang again. Coach Jackson and Karter made the arrangements for a sit-down meeting so the recruiter could persuade him even more to join their organization. Friday, right after school, Karter rushed home as quickly as he could. By three-thirty the recruiter was knocking on his front door.

"Hello Sir! You must be Coach Craig." Karter reached out for a handshake.

"Yes, indeed I am."

"Nice to meet you. Do come in and have a seat."

"How are you?"

"I am doing well, thanks. And you?"

Coach Craig gave a smile, and nodded his head.

"Would you like a cold glass of lemonade or Kool-Aid? My grandmother just prepared it."

"No thanks, Karter. I am fine, thank you. All right, let us get straight to business," Coach Craig said. After they sat down on the couch, Coach Craig opened up his briefcase, and pulled out a brochure of the university. The brochure had bright blue and gold lettering, and it read 'Arizona State University Wildcats' on the front of it. He also pulled out a school application and contract. He laid it down on the living room table. "We have heard and seen a lot of great stories about you man. You are the shit!"

"Really?"

"Yes, the best I have seen by far. We are very interested in you attending our university. Plus, we have the best education, too! Can I ask you something?"

Karter nodded.

"Have you received any other offers from any other schools?" When talking to Coach Craig, Karter gave him direct eye contact. His grandmother taught him giving people direct eye contact showed the highest level of respect. It reflected good manners, and it also meant you were serious and interested about the conversation.

"Oh yeah, Coach Craig! It's very difficult for me right now. I'm trying to figure out which school would be to my best interest. I want to be a superstar. Have you ever wanted something so damned bad that you can just taste it?"

Coach Craig laughed. "Yes, I can relate."

"Well, this is how I feel about football. I am so hungry for it! Since I was a little boy I have been dreaming of this moment. Now it finally has arrived. Do you know graduation is only five months away?"

Coach Craig rubbed his head. "Yes, I am aware of it.

That's why I'd love for you to visit our school's campus for a tour, so we can discuss your future with us. I'll leave this pamphlet of information with you, Karter. Think really hard on a future with us!"

When Coach Craig left the house, Karter thought deeply. He had a huge decision to make. At the same time, it was also very flattering, knowing these prestigious universities were interested in him. And why? Because of his tremendous talent and ability. But only one school would make a huge impact on his future. Which one?

Graduation finally came along.

"Karter Stephens!" the bass voice announced.

Karter looked scholarly in his black cap and gown. As he walked across the stage, he heard the cheers coming from his family and closest friends in the crowd. He accepted his diploma with glee.

"Yay, I did it, Mama!" he said, looking up towards the sky.

Now that high school was finally, over Karter felt more mature and accomplished. Right after high school, some of his friends were enlisting into the military. Some went to college, while others worked nine to five jobs. When he thought about it, it really started to sink in. No more fun, and no more bullshit games. It was kind of depressing, too, just knowing the friendships he established over the three years of high school would not be anymore. It would be so different now, because everyone has to go their separate ways, and enter the real world.

A world of greed; wealthier people grow richer, while the impoverish people stay poorer. Some of his friends would have their heaven on earth, and for some life would turn out to be hell. Moving forward, Karter put the past in the rearview mirror.. His only objective was to become a huge football superstar.

Karter's main concern was to concentrate on making the

right decision. It meant every bit of difference to his career. He rolled up his sleeves and did a lot of research. He weighed his options, and tried to come up with a resolution.

Again, he mumbled the questions to himself. "What school would be good for me and football? Where would my chances be greater at getting drafted into the NFL?"

Karter found out some pertinent information, and he took the tour at the University of Arizona State. He did not want to attend their school. It boiled down to only two schools left, and those two schools were New Mexico and Washington State University. The recruiters at New Mexico State laid it on him heavy, and made him shift his decision from Washington State University to their school.

Karter was sold on New Mexico State University because the recruiters were more convincing than the others. They informed him New Mexico State had not a star quarterback in years, and with him playing for their school, he'd be able to receive recognition, and turn it around for their university, and advance to NFL. Karter loved the sound of it, so he gladly accepted his final offer with the Lobos.

# Game Time

Karter touched down to New Mexico State University, and was ready to take on the world. He had a lot to prove, first, to himself and second, to his family. While waiting in line for his registration he heard the voice of one of his high school English teachers saying, "College would be much tougher than high school."

"Next!"

He walked up to the counter. "Can I help you?" She asked.

"Yes, I would like to complete my registration."

"Okay, what is your first and last name?"

"Karter Stephens!"

She typed on her computer. "Okay, looks like you have a full academic scholarship. Wow... that's awesome!"

"Yes, ma'am, that's correct! I'm here to play football and get a good education."

"Okay, let me print out your classes, and you will be all set."

After finding his dormitory, he examined his room. It was small, cozy, and clean. He was comfortable enough with it, which was good, seeing as he'd be attending the school for four years.

"I wonder who my roommate is," he mumbled under his breath as a young Caucasian man entered the room.

"Hello, are you my roommate?" Karter asked.

"Hello, what's up man. Yes, my name is Greg Miller." Greg reached out to shake Karter's hand.

"I am Karter Stephens! My closest friends call me TQ."

"What does TQ stand for?"

"Too quick."

Greg laughed.

"I am too quick with the football, and not the ladies," Karter said. They laughed.

"Oh, okay. TQ, nice to meet you roomy!"

"Same here, Greg."

"So where are you from man?" Greg asked.

"I'm from Carson, California. I'm here to play football on a scholarship, and I'm going to the NFL."

Greg was shocked because Karter sounded so purposeful. "Wow, sensational man!"

Karter smiled at Greg. "It sounds like you have an accent there. Where are you from?"

Greg busted out into helpless laughter. "I am fronting man. I am from El Paso, Texas. My parents are originally from London though. Every now and then I like to pull people's chain. I like fooling around, you know?"

Karter laughed. "Oh, okay!"

"I'm here to become a heart surgeon."

"Wow, pretty cool man!"

Greg and Karter became more and more acquainted with one another.

They were similar, but also opposites. The one commonality they did share was they each had huge goals and dreams to fulfill. Karter was an athlete with hopes of making it into the NFL, and Greg was a straight-up school nerd with aspirations of becoming a heart surgeon. They were confident young men who spoke passionately of their future careers. In their own worlds, they both had swagger. Greg's appearance and demeanor revealed he came from a wealthy background. His dress code proved it, too. He wore a dark blue turtleneck with an expensive black Versace tailored made suit that fit him to a tee. His shoes were on fleek.

It was not anything like that for Karter. But he tried his

best to remain positive. Life gave Karter lemons, and he was just trying to make some sweet ole lemonade out of it.

Greg walked over to the bed to set his luggage on it. "We will both be working our asses off with the work college has to offer."

"That is fo'sho!" Karter laughed.

"TQ, I'm not too big on partying."

"No party animal here!"

Greg pointed at his chest. "You won't ever have to worry about it getting out of control with me. I am not the sociable type." Greg chuckled.

"I'm so glad to hear, Greg." Karter was relaxed, and cool with Greg. "It looks like we have another thing in common."

Again, the two snickered. They unpacked and settled into their new lives.

The balance between football practices and academic studies became enormously stressful for Karter. College practices were nothing like high school. In high school the practices were two hours long. College practices were four hours longer. During practice he would have to run several laps around the field, lift heavy weights, and do repetitive drills, until the training coach felt it was acceptable for him to stop. He sweated and worked tremendously harder. The only sight he could envision was a shining bright white light at the end of the tunnel, called success. If fans would want to wear Karter's jersey it would be a reflection that he had done something right in his life. Karter had to accept the fact that he would be considered a role model for the universe. It comes along with being a magnificent football superstar. Fame was what he desired and demanded.

The sound of a clock was always in his head. His time was never to be taken for granted or to be wasted. If he wasn't studying, he was practicing his ass off. He did not have any time for partying or anything that would easily distract him from his goal. He wanted to stay focused only on the reason he was in college in the first place: football.

Most players had a special diet to stick to called a training table. A football player could eat whatever food he wanted, as long as there was no pizza, hamburgers, hot dogs, or tacos involved. The coaches wanted their players extra big with weight.

Karter did not have any vices like junk food. He knew they weren't good for his body so he remained clear of them. Playing college football was a huge stepping stone for Karter, and he had to make a lot of sacrifices.

Karter felt the jitters as he paced back and forth along the sideline of the field. What kept going off in his head was he was in college and not high school anymore. It was time for him to produce. Anticipating how it would be his heart pounded faster and faster. He was one step closer to the NFL.

The crowd of fans made their way into the stadium with their nachos, hot dogs, popcorn, and cold drinks in their hands. It was game time!

It was five minutes to kick-off. Karter bowed down and said a quick prayer. "Lord, let me do my thing and be successful tonight. Mom, I hope you are watching me. This is for you!" Looking up into the dark sky, Karter blew a kiss to her. Every time he played; he always thought of his precious mother. He wanted to make her so proud of him.

It was the countdown... ten, nine, eight, seven, six, five, four, three, two, and one.

The New Mexico State players came one by one running out on the field in their silver, red and black uniforms.

"Go, New Mexico... go, New Mexico!" the fans screamed.

Thirty players scampered across the football field breaking the school's banner. On the sideline stood the beautiful cheerleaders who came from every ethnicity. "Let's go New Mexico, let's go!" they cheered.

When halftime rolled around, the young men walked off the field to the locker room.

"The defense is extra tight out there," Coach Craig said. "You guys are playing a great game! I love the energy! Karter, if necessary don't forget you have legs too, so run the ball!"

"Okay, Coach!" Karter smiled and gave him the thumbs up.

"So... let's win, men!" Coach Craig said. "On the count of three. One, two, three... let's win!"

The team shouted along.

Once the guys made it back onto the field, halftime was almost over. Their hyperactive mascot "the wolf" was bouncing up and down, and acting like a buffoon, but hyping up the crowd. The audience laughed at his foolery. Hitting his fist on his chest, Karter took a swig of some lime Gatorade.

"Let's do this!" he yelled.

By the end of the fourth quarter Fresno State was leading the game 22 to 16. The clock was ticking down. The final minutes grew close, until it was fourth quarter with only a minute left on the clock.

The crowd was mostly silent, and at the edge of their seats. "Karter, don't let us down!" A loud, obnoxious fan hollered. Karter surveyed the field, but there wasn't a wide receiver in sight to pass to. So, what could Karter do? He scurried off and dodged to the left. He crept away to the right endzone, managing to avoid every Fresno player. Touchdown! New Mexico won the game. He heard the outpouring of cheers from the fans. The final score was 23 to 22!

After the game Karter hit the shower.

The hot steaming water ran down his firm muscular body, his flesh exhausted from the workout. The heat of the dripping water started to make him relax. It was such an exhilarating feeling. He closed his eyes while enjoying the massage of the water.

He was later surprised by a lady reporter inside of the locker room. He jumped and grabbed a towel to cover his torso. She caught him totally off guard, with only a white towel wrapped around his lower body area. He had the most embarrassing look on his face.

"This is Dana Jenkins from Sports News five! I am standing here with Karter Stephens. First off, congratulations on your win. Awesome game!"

"Thank you!" Karter responded.

"It is incredible how you're able to lift a team to the win. What do you contribute it to?"

Karter gave the reporter direct eye contact. "It is definitely my guys. I have to give credit where credit is due. Being a quarterback, it makes my job a whole lot easier when the guys are open, so I can get the ball to them."

Dana smiled. "Yeah, being a quarterback, you have to be able to take full responsibility for the good, and the bad decisions of the game, right?"

Karter nodded. "Absolutely!"

"When you had to run the ball, what were your thoughts?"

"Dana, at the moment my only thought was making the touchdown, so we could get the victory. I did not want to let my team down, and I was able to do that today. The momentum was there, I was just doing what I do!" Karter laughed. "The win today was for my grandmother Violet."

"Thanks for your time Karter!"

"No problem!" After the interview he continued into the locker room so he could get dressed.

# His Greatest Love

Karter was disgusted and frustrated from a very long, exhausting day of repetitive drills. He'd had to listen to the hollering of Gary, who was one of the meanest and hardest training coaches ever.

"Okay, fellas! Come on over here," Gary shouted.

Karter and Steve, who also played quarterback, jogged over to the sideline.

"What's up, coach?" Karter asked.

"I want you both to run the field. Today, I'm testing for quickness, and afterwards you'll catch and pass," Gary said.

"Okay, coach," Steve said. Karter echoed him.

"When I say go, haul ass to the 100-yard line."

"A'aight," they said together.

"On your mark, get set, go!"

Karter and Steve ran at top speed.

"Run, run, run," Gary yelled.

The sweat dripped down their faces. The race was neck and neck. At 80- yards, Steve began to lead. Karter fell behind a bit. As Steve crossed the 100-yard line, Karter was right behind him, confidence shaken. Confidence played a very important role in performance, and if you lose it, you're unable to perform at your fullest potential.

"Let's do it over, again! Faster, faster, faster!" Gary's hand-clapping, got louder and louder. "Hustle, hustle, hustle!" And again, Steve won.

When it came to practice, Gary did not bullshit. Gary was the sternest out of all the coaching staff and when he looked at Karter, Karter knew he meant business. On this day, Gary was really riding Karter's ass.

"No, it's not good enough!" He blew the whistle. "Nope, do it again! What is wrong with you today, Karter? You sick, tired or something man?"

"Nah, I am good!" Karter said. But deep down inside he was feeling frustrated. And although Gary was super strict, Karter could not get upset with his style of training. As the old saying went: practice makes perfect. Karter wanted to be the best quarterback he possibly could be. But when Coach Gary threw a swift pass to him, he missed it.

"It's just not my fucking day!" he whispered under his breath. "What the hell else could go wrong?"

As he looked around Coach John signaled, waving his arm in the air, so he could get Karter's to come over to the sideline.

"Yeah, coach? What's up?"

"I just received a message, and you need to call your Aunt Kerrie, as soon as possible."

Karter looked puzzled. "Did she say why?"

"No, but by the tone of her voice it seemed very urgent. You better go call her right now!"

Karter looked mystified. "Okay, thanks, Coach John!" Karter rushed to the nearest pay phone to make the call. It was unusual for his Aunt Kerrie to call during football practice.

"Hello?"

"Hello, Aunt Kerrie, what's going on out there? How are you?"

Aunt Kerrie did not answer the question. Instead, she asked, "How is it going out there, Karter?"

"It's all good, Aunt Kerrie!" he said. "I just finished wrapping up football practice. If I sound a little out of breath it is only because I am training really hard." Karter rubbed a towel across his forehead to catch the dripping sweat. "What's up, Aunt Kerrie?"

She inhaled and then exhaled.

"Why do you sound so distraught?" he asked.

"Karter, I am so sorry. I hate to call you and have to tell you this, but I have a bit of bad news for you." Frantically, she started crying.

"Oh no, Aunt Kerrie... what's wrong?" "Is everybody okay?"

Aunt Kerrie said, "No. You know your grandmother had been ill for some time now. Well today she passed onto heaven."

"Oh, no! Nooooo!" His heart felt broken, shattered into a thousand pieces.

Aunt Kerrie tried to console him. "Listen to me! Your grandmother was taking chemotherapy and radiation treatments, but her cancer progressed rapidly. It is better this way. No more suffering and no more pain, right?"

Karter was absolutely speechless.

"Today, she went onto be with the Lord and your mother."

With a sigh, he asked, "So when is the funeral?"

"We're planning the memorial service for next Saturday, at eleven o'clock in the morning."

Karter made no sound.

"Karter, are you still there?"

"Yes, I am here. I was thinking about my schedule. Okay, I have a game against Norte Dame at ten o'clock next Saturday. But I will have to cancel, without a doubt I will be there!"

After hanging up the telephone, Karter kicked the locker so hard it left a supersized dent. Tears ran down his face. After a few minutes, he was able to regain his composure. He reflected on his memories of his grandmother. The good, bad, and the ugly times.

Instantly, he could smell the aroma of her cooking. It was always so delicious. Her voice he could clearly hear saying, "Karter, Flip, and Tiff, get your butts in this house!"

as she would often say, right before the street lights came on.

Like the color and flower, her name was Violet. She had been a special woman whose heart was as genuine as gold. The kind of person who would never leave you in the cold. Violet's words could warm your soul. Her personality was sincere and never phony, but she always made herself clear. Not trying to be what she was not. She would give up her very last dollar to you. Violet would make you laugh, and holler right out of your seat. The words to sum her up is a spirit so unique.

Someone who you definitely do not meet in this crazy world twice. A simply phenomenal woman who was so nice! Karter's grandmother was his greatest love. The outpouring chuckles would come out of her mouth. When she watched the television show Mash. She really loved Mash! Violet was a strong woman. Her demeanor was laid back and cool. She taught her grandchildren how to be their best. Guiding her young grandsons into becoming strong leaders as men, and her granddaughters into becoming strong women. She did her absolute best on shaping them into productive citizens. Even when the funds were low, and the debts were high. The motto she followed, "Where there is a will there is a way?"

Karter reflected back on his childhood. How in the hell had she been able to raise them? "How did you do it, grandma?" he muttered. He looking up to the heavens. "Thank you for raising us, and everything you have done for me. Because of you, I am the man I am today!"

Karter blew a kiss in the air. "I love you, grandma!" He yelled. "Im going to miss you! Rest in peace!"

After the funeral, Karter constantly grieved. It was extremely difficult to carry on with his life, but he still worked relentlessly. He wanted to make his grandmother so proud of him. Now that she was gone, success would not exactly feel the same. Karter prepared himself for his final exams. He studied so diligently it would give him intense headaches.

The time had rushed by. He glanced over at the calendar. Graduation had come and gone as well as the entire school year, and still Karter had not been drafted into the NFL. Some coaches had their reasons why Karter did not make it to the NFL. One being, he was not tall enough. According to New Mexico State's coaching staff, six feet and four inches was the prototype for an NFL quarterback. Karter stood out at six feet, and some inches. Weighing two-hundred and seventy-five pounds. There were always going to be players faster and more athletic.

# A Black Man's Disappointment

The year was nineteen ninety-two. President George W.H. Bush was in office, and the economy was shitty. Karter walked into the elevator with a bounce in his step and every care on his solitary mind. At times, his only downfall was that he could be naïve. He believed what people told him without deciphering the truth for himself. The real world was frigid, and it was beginning to become a whole lot chillier for Karter Stephens. It was a cruel kind of world, different from his college days. It was about making the dollar bills. Karter applied for his very first accounting position. He walked into the building and up to the information desk.

"Hello, I am here to apply for the accounting position."

A security guard pointed his finger, and directed him to the eleventh floor. "Yes, right that way, sir!"

Karter's heart raced as he strolled into the elevator. The interview was scheduled for ten o'clock in the morning. He looked down to check the time on his Fossil watch. It was nine forty-five exactly. He arrived fifteen minutes early to make a good first impression. Punctuality was always a must! Once he walked off the elevator, every eye was focused on him. At a desk sat a white lady wearing glasses hanging down her nose. She worked at a Dell computer. Her name tag read 'Carol'. Karter went to the desk.

"Good Morning, Carol. I have a ten o'clock interview with Julie."

Carol gaped at him in surprise. "Oh, okay," she replied.

"How many positions are there?" Karter asked.

"We are seeking one qualified candidate for the

position."

He was flabbergasted. "Only one?"

"Yes, just one. Please have a seat and fill out the application. Julie will be with you shortly!"

"Thank you," he said. Karter grabbed the clipboard with the application attached to it and took a seat. He looked around to become familiar with those applying for the same position. Five men were already seated and filling out their applications. Two were Caucasian, two were Asian, and one was Hispanic. For that one job! His grandmother's voice went off in his head.

"Because you are black, you are going to have to work like hell. Twice as hard... no matter what!" Karter had been taught competition on the football field, but the corporate world felt totally different. His confidence had hit the floor. He felt extremely incompetent. He was agitated, and he kept looking around feeling nervous. While filling out his application, Karter kept focused on his competition. He felt more and more uncomfortable. Being an accountant was known as an occupation mostly for white men. He was the only black man waiting in the reception area. Football had prepared him for competition on the field, and college prepared him for accounting, but he was unprepared for the competition he would face at job interviews. Karter contemplated the situation. Did he even have what it takes to be there in the first place?

He kept doubting himself and his abilities. Julie suddenly walked inside from a side corridor. She was running a little late, so she picked up her pace. When she made it within close range the look on her face expressed it. She thought, *Oh, my gosh! He is black!*

Karter spoke very eloquently; his dialect was always proper. He fooled most employers over the telephone. They would automatically assume he was Caucasian. When interview day came it was always a surprising revelation.

Face to face, Julie was shocked because she was used to interviewing mostly Caucasian men for the positions. She tried to play it off, but it was rather noticeable. She extended her hand, and greeted Karter with a hesitant handshake, as though he had cooties or something. She coughed and cleared her throat. Just maybe Julie had a flashback into time. When she was teased by little black Billy at school or maybe the time, she had just finished shopping at the mall, and a black man wrapped his arms around her neck robbing her at gun point.

She appeared agitated. "Hello, I'm Julie!"

Karter acted oblivious to what was happening right in front of him. He felt awkward, and she looked awkward. "Hello, I'm Karter Stephens."

"Hi Karter, it is a pleasure to meet you." Pretending everything was all right, she gave him a deceiving smile.

"Same here Julie," he smiled back.

"Please follow me." She said. They walked to a side office so Julie could conduct the interview. Julie asked, "What college did you attend?"

"New Mexico State," he said proudly.

"So, Karter tell me about yourself and why you want the position."

Karter felt uneasy, but he gave a brief description of himself. He assured her, "I'm good with numbers, and because I really need a job!" he said.

Julie gave him a peculiar, unimpressed look.

"Do you have your accounting degree and resume?" she asked.

"Yes, I sure do." Karter handed his resume to her.

"Ummm, impressive." Julie said, her voice flat. "Karter, for this position it is mandatory we have five job references."

He looked confused, because it had not stated that in the Daily Breeze newspaper.

"I just graduated from college, so how am I going to

have five job refences?"

"I am sorry, Karter," she said. "We're looking for an accountant with five years of experience and work history." Her voice held a note of condescension.

"What?" Karter asked. "Five years of work history, too?"

Julie nodded. "Yes, at least five years of work history!"

Karter looked skeptical.

"I have a few more candidates to interview."

"But-" Karter interrupted.

Julie repeated. "I have two more interviews today, and I will have my decision by the end of the week."

Karter rose and shook her hand. Even though he held a degree in accounting he felt like he was being treated as though he didn't have one. Karter felt humiliated and stupid.

After he left the office, Julie felt safer. She then threw his resume in the trash can. "Good, he is finally gone," she said.

Karter left the building with his pride stripped away. He walked away disappointed and frustrated, feeling less than a man. His spirit was low as the ground. He thought about the in-depth conversation he would have with Queenie. He contemplated and prepared himself for the hundred and one questions she would ask. They called her Queenie because like a queen she carried herself in the highest manner. She had smooth, light butterscotch skin. She sported blonde highlights in her asymmetrical long bob, and she had a smile that could make your heart melt. In addition to her magnificent beauty she was both book and street smart.

Queenie was in the same position as Karter. She was looking for a gig too. Queenie dreamt of becoming a sultry movie star. Becoming famous was at the top of her list. She felt she had deep talents resonating within her. The entertainment business was a tough business to get into. So, Queenie worked several jobs that did not give her any type of fulfillment. She was in an awkward position; it seemed like a finger had pushed the pause button on her life. Her career path was nebulous. Queenie did not like working a job, but she had to do it until, she could get to where she really wanted to be in her life. The phone was ringing, when Karter opened the door. Queenie was extremely curious about Karter's interview. She could not wait to hear his good news.

"Hello," he said.

"So how did it go?"

"Queenie, it was all good." Despite his lie, Karter had a disturbing look on his face.

"Really, TQ? You don't sound too assertive about it, if it was all good."

Karter felt he had to tell her the truth. "Honestly, Queenie? Fuck! I don't feel too positive about the interview. Those stares and the way Julie the interviewer made me feel. She made me feel illiterate, or something. It was a very humiliating experience, Queenie."

"Really? What a bitch, dude! So, what are you saying, TQ?"

"The company had a requirement of five job references and work history. I just graduated."

"Did they list it in the ad?" she asked.

"No! Life is so fucking unfair!"

"Yeah, I know, man. Life is not fair!" Queenie sat there thinking, and like an investigator she started to put the pieces altogether. "Anyways, sounds like discrimination to me. Some vicious people will say just about anything to try to discourage you."

"Oh, yeah! Queenie, it's exactly how I felt. The system is wacked! Some people bust their ass their whole entire life and still have little or nothing to show for it. I have seen it before, within my very own family."

"Oh, TQ you are absolutely right, I know. I am so sorry

for your terrible experience!" Queenie said. "Yeah, it is definitely a screwed-up system and a cruel world, but eventually things will get better for you. Don't worry, I promise. It's a trial period. Watch, you will see. When things don't work out the way you anticipate, it is because God has a bigger plan for you. You have to keep the faith and trust his plan for your life. Maaaan, just don't give up though!" Queenie always encouraged Karter, though it may have been deeper than even she could imagine.

"Let's go look for some more jobs tomorrow," Queenie said. "You'll get one soon. Don't stress out over it."

When Karter heard Queenie's kind words of inspiration, he felt relieved, as though ten pounds of weights lifted off his shoulder. Queenie believed in him even when he did not believe in himself. "Thanks, Queenie! I really needed to hear that. I despise this feeling of rejection and unclarity in my life."

"Like I said before, TQ. Things will get better! All right, I have to go now. I'm out."

"Okay, talk to you later Queenie!"

Since high school, Queenie and Karter been close buddies. Nothing romantic, just close friends. No matter what the situation, their friendship was tight as a rubber band.

Karter and Queenie applied with many more companies. Some large, some small. They dropped off their resumes all over town, knocked on every door imaginable. But the doors kept slamming in their faces expeditiously. At this point it began to feel like the four years of college was a total waste of Karter's time and energy. Most people thought that when you attended and graduate from a prestigious university you are guaranteed a great career. They assumed you will make a ton of money. Karter had thought so too, but a good high paying career was looking pretty bleak right about now. Karter and Queenie continued on with their job search.

One Wednesday, Karter walked into a KFC. "I see the sign out front says you are accepting applications," He said.

"Yes, we sure are!" the manager said. "We're looking for cooks. Do you have any cooking experience?"

Karter said, shamefaced, "No, but I have a lot of years of cash handling experience. Do you need a very qualified cashier? Here is my resume."

When Karter handed over his resume the manager was shocked. "Oh, my gosh! You are a graduate of the University of New Mexico. Congratulations! Why are you applying here?"

"Man, I need a job!"

"You are well over-qualified. This job only pays $5.25 an hour. We can't afford to pay you what you deserve."

"Anyways, shit!" Karter snapped, snatched his resume back, and stormed out the door.

Life had dealt Karter a hand of bad cards. He felt terrible about being rejected from every accounting position he had applied for. But what could he do?

Sometimes, he got nervous and choked up. Often, he sold himself short to interviewers. Also, the economy was in a terrible state, and being a black educated man in America was not the easiest. He dealt with prejudice and discrimination. Some people could be so judgmental with their stereotypes. Karter started to have second and even third thoughts about his career choice. Constantly doubting himself, because it was so extremely difficult for him to get his foot inside any corporate door. He knocked and knocked, but no one would open the door. He knocked again, and still no one answered. No company would hire Karter and give him the opportunity he so well deserved. Unfortunately, life didn't always work out the way we would like it to. It became cold, dark, and lonely. Karter's sadness kicked in with a vengeance.

"Ha! Ha! Ha! Hello Karter," it said in a villainous satanic voice. Karter was alone, and in complete darkness, searching, but unable to find a way out of a pitch-dark black hole. It kept pulling and sucking him in even deeper. It took him spiraling downward. Karter tried to break away free from it, but he was hypnotized and under its spell. He was sinking lower and lower without any control.

# Depression

Karter was asleep when the telephone rung. "Hello," he mumbled.

"What are you doing?" Queenie asked.

"What's up, Queenie! I'm chilling. I think I am trying to catch a cold."

Karter sounded so depressed to her, like Eeyore. "I hope you are not still tripping over that job interview, man."

"Nah, actually I'm good!"

Queenie knew he was lying. "Okay, yeah right!"

"Nah, for real, Queenie. I am not worried about the interview. It's the job search that has me bothered."

"TQ, I know it can be a bit draining. Especially when you have bills to pay. We can hit up some more companies tomorrow. I heard Pac Bell is looking for an accountant."

"Word?"

"Yeah, for real! Let's go early in the morning. The early bird catches the worm," Queenie said. Her father had always told her growing up.

"All right, sounds like a plan." Karter said. "See you tomorrow Queenie!"

Karter and Queenie hunted and hunted, hoping to find a good paying job. It was the sign of the times, with escalating unemployment, inflation, high crime, and homelessness. Damn this life! But Karter's faith hit an all-time high. He started to question God a lot more. He couldn't comprehend why it was so difficult for him to catch a break. Karter grew closer and closer to God, but encountered a lot of moments when he felt as though God were punishing him for some unknown sin.

"Oh Lord, why am I having such a tough time in my life? Please forgive me for whatever I may have done wrong!" He prayed and prayed his situation would finally turn around for the better. After several consistent prayers to the big almighty man above he finally received a break.

It was an ordinary day in the spring time. A sunny eighty degrees with a light ocean breeze that swayed the trees from side to side. Karter was filled with disgust, and pretty much damn near at the end of his rope.

"Fuck!" he said.

It was his favorite profanity word. Normally, he did not answer the telephone in the early mornings, because he thought it was a friend asking for money, a favor, or probably just another desperate bill collector trying to collect their funds, but this time he did answer it.

"Hello, who's dis?

"Hello, may I please speak to Karter Stephens?" The woman's diction was professional, and he cleared his throat, changing the way he spoke.

"Yes, this is he. And how may I help you?"

"My name is Mary. How are you?"

"Good, ma'am!" he replied with a smile, voice cheerful.

"Great," Mary said. "You applied with our company about a month, ago right?"

"Yes."

"Are you still interested in the position?"

"Yes, I am very much interested!"

"Okay, great," she said. "I am conducting interviews. By chance are you available today?"

When he heard 'today', he became overjoyed. "Yes, that works for me!"

"Can you come in at two o'clock?"

"Yes! Yes! Yes!" he responded anxiously. "Yes, I can interview today at two."

"Okay," Mary said, and laughed. "All right, we'll see you at two o'clock, Karter!"

"See you then, Mary." After he hung up the telephone, he dashed to the closet so he could pick out his business attire. Karter chose a black peak lapel business suit, a white dress shirt, black tie, and a pair of shiny black patent leather shoes. Once he finished getting dressed, he looked in the mirror.

"Ooh, la la." he said.

While preparing himself mentally two o'clock was fast approaching. On the drive, he said another quick prayer. "Dear God, I know you're aware of my struggles. I ask of you to please pull me through and let me be victorious today. I am financially stressed out. I am drowning in my debt and sinking underwater. I am fed up with my life! My worries I turn over to you. Please let the right words flow out of my being. Help me to be triumphant today. In your son Jesus' name, amen!"

Karter's hair was neatly groomed and he was well dressed. He looked very distinguished. His brut cologne smelled very masculine and wonderful. He strutted into the building like John Travolta in *Staying Alive*. You couldn't tell him shit. Nothing, not a damn thing! He was overconfident, and feeling like a superstar. This time around everyone was so extremely busy in the office no one even paid any attention to him. When he walked up to the front desk, where there sat a black woman who seemed to really dislike her job. According to her name tag her name was Felicia. Felicia was on the telephone, so he waited patiently. After waiting a few more minutes she finally hung up.

Smacking her lips, her tone held attitude. "Hello, how can I help you?"

"Hi, yes, I am here to see Mary. I have a two o'clock interview."

"Okay, one moment. Just have a seat and I will buzz her to let her know you are here." Felicia said snappily. Karter arrived exactly on time. It was two o'clock sharp, so he took a seat in the lobby. He picked up an Essence magazine and killed a little time as he waited. Twenty minutes went by. He then picked up a Jet magazine and continued reading. Karter started to get really aggravated, but he still waited as patiently as he could. He sat in the reception area, thinking about the rules of punctuality, and he felt it should be mutual for corporate America to be on time too. He became very restless. He leaned his head back for a brief second, and closed his eyes. All of a sudden Mary appeared right before him.

"Hello. You must be Karter."

"Yes, how are you?" he said. Karter stood.

"I am doing well, and thank you for asking," she said. "I am Mary. It's nice to meet you!"

"Likewise!" he said. Karter gripped Mary's hand, and they exchanged a firm handshake.

"I am so sorry for my tardiness. We had an employee who just up and quit on us, and without a two-week notice too. Some people have no respect at all. Just resigned out of nowhere." Mary shook her head. "So, we are so swamped with work.

Karter was ecstatic to hear that. If he qualified for the position, it could mean he could be offered the job right on the spot. With direct eye contact Karter stared at Mary. He wanted to show his level of respect, and let her know he was really interested in the position. "Wow, really?" he asked.

They walked to a nice and quiet secluded room located in the very rear end of the building. Mary seemed overwhelmed, and it was obvious she was extremely stressed out. She took a deep breath. "Do you have a resume?"

"Oh, yes I do." Karter pulled out his resume from his black briefcase and handed it to her. "Here it is."

Mary started reading. "So tell me a little about yourself."

"Well, I am a graduate from New Mexico State with a bachelor's degree in accounting. I am dependable, hardworking, and a team player." He represented himself with such dignity, and spoke articulately, so he could assure her. This time around Karter felt extremely comfortable. He was unnerved, because Mary gave off a different type of energy.

"I am very impressed!" she said. "By the way, congratulations! It's not easy, finishing college. It takes a lot of discipline and hard work. I applaud you for it."

Because of Karter's hard work and track record Mary made a decision. "Karter, I'm so inspired by you. I am hiring you right on the spot! When can you start working?"

"Immediately!" he said. Karter wore a huge smile on his face.

"Okay, sounds great!" Mary smiled. "I will see you on Monday at 8 a.m. sharp." They shook hands, and Karter was on his way.

He rushed home and called Queenie.

"Hello?" Her voice sounded groggy because she had just woken up.

"Queenie, I got the job!"

"Really? That's great news, TQ! I knew you would get one soon. We have to celebrate this wonderful occasion. It's on me!"

"Sounds good!" Karter said. "Thanks for not letting me give up, friend."

"What are friends for?"

"Okay... Talk to you later Queenie."

"Alright, bye TQ!"

When Karter got off the telephone, he looked up. "Thank you, God, for looking out for me today!"

Every day at work was going swell. Karter liked his new position and the work environment. Especially the fact he would be earning income again. It was truly a blessing from above… until the problems started to arise within his reports. *Most cases, this is the dynamics of a job*, he thought. *It seems like things are always good until you hit the ninety-day probationary period, right?*

This is when all hell broke loose for Karter. He was summoned by his manager Debbie.

"Hello, Karter this is Debbie. Can I see you in my office please?"

He sat there baffled for a couple of minutes. He wondered what was the problem? There was only thirty minutes left on the time clock. Before his shift was going to be over. He entered Debbie's office; the uncertainty started rushing through his mind. "Yes, Debbie you wanted to see me?"

"Yes, Karter. Please have a seat. How is it going?" she asked.

"It's going well, and I really love it here." Karter said, and smiled.

"That's great. Well, I brought you in here today because unfortunately there have been a few complaints in accounts receivable. There seems to be some inaccuracies on some of the reports. I wanted to bring it to your attention so you can address it, and make any necessary corrections." She pulled out the reports, and pointed out his red highlighted circled errors. After doing so she congratulated him. "Congratulations on your ninety days with the company!"

"I would like to evaluate your ninety-day job performance."

"Okay!" Karter smiled.

"First of all, your attendance has been impeccable. Your work ethic and attitude have been excellent! We have no complaints in that department. The only problem is there were just a few mistakes on the reports, but it's nothing that can't be corrected. Since you have looked over your errors, please sign this document. This written document will be placed in your file."

Karter looked over his errors. "Debbie, I want to apologize for the discrepancies, and I will stay focused."

Debbie smiled. "Do you have any further questions?"

Karter smiled back. "No, it's clear to me."

"Okay, as long as we are clear and on the same page, we're all good! You will be receiving a fifty-cent raise on your next paycheck."

"Thank you!" Karter was excited.

"If you don't have any other questions our meeting is now adjourned."

Karter wanted to believe he was ecstatic with his new job. It was a second chance, a whole new beginning. But truth be told, he kept reflecting on the past. Deep down inside, he felt rebellious towards the world because of how life turned out for him. Working as an accountant was not exactly what he wanted to be doing with his life. Instead, he much rather wanted to be a football superstar. He kept thinking of his dreams, all of his hard work, and what he had achieved. The preparation and dedication gone quickly swirling down the drain. The thoughts of it made him become even angrier.

When the nightfall came, he tossed and turned. Entangled in his comforter in his bed, he struggled to fall asleep. Every day and night, he fought with the nightmare of reality. Dreams of himself passing the football flashed into his unconsciousness. He desperately tried to block it out, but reality set in. The memories of high school, his college days of practicing, plus being rejected from the NFL were locked into his mentality. Karter's mind so wrapped around becoming a football superstar he was now completely lost, and because of this he slipped back into that cold, dark, and lonely place. He started to dabble with alcohol only to soothe his pain of rejection, but before he knew it the problems arose on the job again.

The spreadsheet reports had several inconsistencies with the numbers. The figures just were not adding up correctly. There was a buzz on the intercom again. Karter began to get really anxious. This time the voice erupting through the line was very hostile. "As soon as possible, can I please see you in my office?"

His heart raced. Balancing the rejection of football along with keeping the records of a prestigious company had begun to take a tremendous toll on him mentally and spiritually. The weight of the pressure overpowered his mind. It felt like it was driving him insane. At times, he felt as if he was going to have a mental breakdown. A few months passed on only to find himself right back in the same position.

Karter slowly walked into the office. This was the third strike! "Yes, you wanted to see me Debbie?"

"Yes, I do," Debbie said. "Please have a seat. I've been looking over the spreadsheets, and there are some more miscalculations.

"Again, really?" Karter looked dumbfounded.

"Karter, are you all right?"

"Yes, I'm fine. Thanks," he stuttered. "Why do you ask?"

Debbie reached inside her desk for a red pen. "Because these inaccuracies are simple boo-boos. It is the basics! By the way, I received a few other complaints about your tardiness too. Some of your co-workers noticed you have been acting a little weird and unlike yourself lately. They said it seems like you are in a different world."

"Really?" Karter looked bewildered. "Yes, Debbie, I'll admit life does have a way of taking a toll on you. Lately I've been under a little stress. I have a few health issues that I am experiencing."

"I hope it's not anything serious. Is it?" Debbie gave him a sympathetic look.

"No, it's not anything major with me, Debbie." By this

point, Karter felt a little angry.

Debbie looked confounded. "Do you want to talk about it?"

"Nah, I'm good. Thank you, I really appreciate your concern," Karter said.

"Well, this is how we are going to handle this situation. I have another document for you to look over and sign. Karter, once you've read it please sign here." Debbie pointed to the dotted line on the document.

"This report states we did address the occurrence at hand." He quickly read it and signed on the dotted line. "Karter this is your last and final warning. If you get one more of these we will have no other choice but to terminate your position with us!"

When Karter heard the word terminate, he lost total control. His nerves started to tremble; it was like he was having a seizure. His rage grew stronger, and he wanted to be destructive, and rip up some shit. Karter couldn't believe the conversation he'd just had. He got up out of his seat and exited Debbie's office, feeling resentment and confusion. He took a deep breath and tried to regain his composure. He started inhaling and exhaling. "One, two, three, four, five, six, seven, eight, nine, and ten," he counted. This was an exercise he learned in Health and Behavioral class in college. "How to Relieve Stress and Anger by Breathing." Whenever he became pissed or stressed out he would use this technique.

With the threat of termination, he became even more self-conscious about every move he made. Working at the company was like walking on pins and needles. Most of the time, Karter felt edgy, discouraged, and unsure of himself. If he screwed up one more time, he would be fired.

Some months passed, only for Karter to find himself back in the same predicament.

"Hey, Karter."

"Hi, Debbie."

"Can I please talk to you a minute?"

He stopped calculating his numbers. "Yeah, what's happening?"

"I want to show you something." From a manila folder, Debbie pulled out his paperwork. Karter had a here-we-go-again look on his face. "We found more faults in your work."

Shaking his head, he said, "No, how could it be? Debbie, I have been really careful with my figures."

"Are you sure?" Debbie said.

Karter looked mystified. "Yes, I am positive!"

"See, look here." Debbie pointed out his slip-ups. He shrank down into his seat. He felt extremely flustered. "I really hate to do this, but I am going to have to terminate you."

"No, C'mon! Please give me one more chance, Debbie. Please, I promise it won't happen again. I will get it right, I promise!" He said.

"I am sorry, Karter!" Debbie handed him his last two-weeks' paycheck.

"Okay, fine then!" He snatched it.

"I will give you a minute to clear your desk," She said.

While Karter gathered his belongings, he fumed. He thought, *what do I do next?* It meant being right back in the unemployment line to find another job. He despised the process of trying to find work all over again. Karter had developed an enormous chip on his shoulder, blaming people and the world for where he was in his life. Often he felt like he was ready to explode.

# They Meet Interracially

After months of stressing to the fullest, Karter was finally able to find another job. His world was good, but he was missing out on one thing in his life: love. So he decided to check out a nearby club scene. There she was, standing by the bar, radiant and fine. Fluorescent purple and blue flashing lights shone on her brightly. The explicit version of Prince's song *Erotic City* was blasting from the sound system. She bobbed her head to the music.

The vibration of the music were loud enough to make a *house quake.* What a *beautiful one! S*he stood at five feet even. Her hair was blonde, and her eyes were blue. She was wearing a *pink cashmere hot dress w*ith fishnet black panty hose, all of which accented her curvaceous body. While there were plenty of other gorgeous women dancing on the floor, they couldn't compare to this woman.

Because of her sophisticated look, Karter did a doubletake. Staring at her body and being pulled by the bait, Karter paid close attention to only her. This lady was definitely unique in her own fashionable style, unlike the thots who were twerking on the dance floor, one of whom approached him.

"Excuse me! *If I was your girlfriend,"* she said. She handed Karter her phone number. "Call me *if you want a funky time!"*

*She* looked him up and down with her ass was hanging out of her clothes. Disgusted by her appearance, Karter looked at her and just shook his head. "Sorry, I'm waiting on my date to arrive," he said. "Anyways, man, you aren't my type!"

She stumbled off, visibly drunk. Karter was uninterested in that kind of woman. His eyes were still focused on the lady sitting at the bar. She represented true elegance. What a classy dame! *Betcha by golly, wow!* Karter started singing, "You are the one I have been waiting for forever." He looked at her with such strong conviction in his eyes, as if to say she was *the most beautiful girl in the world.* Her confidence was undeniable, and her body was banging like a fucking *tambourine.* Karter vibed to her music. Along with being spellbound by this woman's captivating presence, Karter was mesmerized and completely under her spell. Love was sexy, and it was definitely in the air!

Drawn to her like a magnet, Karter was pulled in closer because of her daring beauty. Intrigued, he walked over with swagger to pursue her. A sensation shot through his entire body. It was obvious he truly *adored* her appearance.

"Hey, *you got the* look!" he said. "I could not help but notice you from across the room. I had to meet you! You are so beautiful!"

She blushed. "Thank you!" she said.

"This may seem straight and forward, but *I want to be your lover.*"

She laughed at his candidness and aggressiveness.

"I had to be totally honest with you! What is your name, gorgeous?"

"My name is Nikki," she chuckled. Nikki was very moved by his charisma. "What is your name?"

"Darlin, I'm Karter! It's a pleasure to meet you!" Reaching out for her hand, he kissed it. When it was necessary he knew how to be a gentleman. His grandmother taught him how to be charming and respectful to a woman. "Can I buy you a drink?"

"Yes, thank you!" She nodded. "A Shirley Temple is fine!"

"Only a Shirley Temple?" he asked.

She gave him a look.

"Okay, a Shirley Temple it is." They shared a laugh.

"I don't normally drink alcohol," she said.

"Oh, okay! So, do you come here often?" Karter asked.

"No, I am celebrating with my girl. She is about to get married."

"Oh, okay! That's nice," Karter said.

"Do you come here a lot?" she asked.

"Nah, I just needed to get out. I have been going through it. I had to get out and have some fun, you know?"

"Yeah, I feel you."

Karter stared deeply into her eyes. "I am really glad to meet you lady!"

"Nice to meet you too! So where are you from?" Nikki asked.

"Carson, Cali," Karter said. "I came to New Mexico for college football, and after graduating I decided to make it home."

"Ooh, okay," Nikki said.

"Where are you from?" he asked.

"I was born and raised here. After high school I got a 9 to 5 working as a secretary. Immediately moved out of my parents' house because they were bugging."

"Okay." Karter laughed.

"Can I get you two some drinks?" the bartender asked.

"Yes, bartender! A Shirley Temple for the beautiful lady, and a Cadillac Margarita for me.

"Coming right up!"

"Thank you." Karter's eyes were back on Nikki again. "I can't stop saying it. You are so attractive!"

"Thank you!" Nikki seemed extremely flattered at Karter's charm and respectfulness, but at the same time, she had heard it so many times before. Some men could be so monotonous, and about the same ole bullshit. And for Nikki it wasn't about the talk, only about actions.

The bartender arrived. "Okay, sir, that'll be thirty dollars."

"Here you go, man." Karter handed him a fifty-dollar bill.

"I'll be right back with your change."

"No, keep the change," he said.

Nikki looked very impressed. When a man tips the waiter big, it meant he appreciated the lady's company and he wanted to fascinate her.

"I want to make a toast." Karter raised his glass, Nikki raised hers. "To new friendships."

"To new friendships," she repeated. They lightly tapped their glasses.

Nikki had been propositioned by many men. Some married, straight, and even bisexual, but the chemistry with Karter was so strong. Nikki's eyes scoped him on the sly. His appearance was what most women would desire in a man. Karter was sweet eye-candy. As a kid, it looked like he could have worn braces. His teeth were pearly white and super straight. He had a long-pointed nose, light-colored brown eyes, and smooth clear skin. What a *sexy motherfucker!* They finished sipping their drinks. "Sweetie, may I have this dance?" Karter asked.

"Yes!" her *soft and wet* voice replied. Walking to the dance floor, they danced the night away. They partied like it was *1999*. Her dance moves were so smooth, like a *stripper or a sexy dancer. Nikki was enticing Karter with her body.* They were enjoying each other's company, but what stood out the most about Karter, *he was black.*

The year was 2011, and interracial dating was the happening thing, a long way from the days of segregation in *America*. At first Nikki was a little skeptical, but she played it off.

"So, what's your phone number?" Karter asked.

She replied, "*777-9311.*"

He wrote it down. "Okay, I'm going to call you!" She winked. Karter folded up Nikki's phone number and put it inside his pocket.

The anticipation of what was to come for the both of them was the unknown. In the beginning it was like any normal relationship. When they saw each other, they felt butterflies. They both would feel that *let's go crazy* feeling when they were not near one another. Getting off the telephone in the wee hours of the morning, usually one or two o'clock. Karter and Nikki were inseparable. They showed all the signs of *when two are in love.* Love is love, and it dwelled inside of their hearts. The three questions Nikki wondered about were: is it true what they said about black men? Was Karter's penis size large enough to make her *gettoff,* and could he work it in the bedroom? More importantly, was he paid? He had his questions and reservations too. For instance, could she be sweet and cater to a man's needs sexually? Could she be a lady in the streets, and was she the freaky type of woman in the bedroom who loved many sexual positions? Soon time would reveal the answers to their questions. When it came to sex, neither were virgins. This time around dating someone of a different race would be totally different. They wanted to get to know each other's backgrounds. For example, how did they grow up? Their different cultures and beliefs. After spending a lot time together, they became *insatiable.* Never getting enough of each other. Two people crazy in love into one another like a hand in a glove.

It got to the point, they wanted to be totally exclusive. She located a nice spot in Arizona, and they made the long distant move from New Mexico to Arizona. The first few months were lovey-dovey. Some months later, Nikki became super lazy. She stopped going to work. The bills accumulated.

When Karter came home from a long exhausting day at

work, it was pitch dark in their apartment. He flicked the switch but the lights would not come on.

"What in the hell is going on?" Karter asked. Nikki pretended to have forgotten to pay the bill. She was lying on the couch with a flashlight in her hand and reading over the electric bill. In reality, she didn't have any money to pay the bill.

"Hey Sunshine, what's going on?" he asked again.

She gave him a pitiful look. "Oops. I'm sorry, my love! I didn't have any money to pay the bill."

"Damn it! Girl, what the hell is wrong with you?" Karter scratched his head. "Yesterday, I gave you money, so you could! Do you remember? I even reminded you the bill was due today."

Nikki just glanced at him. "I know you did Karter, but I had to pay another bill with that money."

"Are you serious? Damn it, what happened to the money, Sunshine?"

"I spent it. Never mind!" she said.

Karter was so livid he grabbed her by the arm. "What? For real? Did you buy more clothes, huh?" Nikki just looked at him. "Girl, you have a serious problem."

Nikki looked down and then up like a puppy being scolded. "Yeah, the only problem I have is I want to look good for you all the time!"

Karter was shocked. "For me?"

"Yes, for you!" she said. "Honey, don't worry! First thing in the morning, I will take care of it." She gave him a juicy kiss to reassure him. "I promise... I'll take care of it!"

The next day came and Nikki managed to pay the electric bill. Within a few weeks, it occurred again, this time the telephone and the cable. Karter had become disgusted with Nikki being so irresponsible, and her nonchalant ways. She started to take everything very lightly. She was taking Karter for granted. The financial pressures put a tremendous strain on their now *strange relationship*. It seemed as though Nikki would only do things to annoy Karter. She didn't want to see him happy, but at the same time she hated to see him sad. She was a little confused about love. She hung out more with her friends, and constantly shopped. Because of it more arguments came profusely.

Nikki went from being a career ambitious woman, to a woman who became dependent on Karter. Healthwise her body was willing and *able to work, but* one morning she just woke up and decided she did not want to go to work anymore. "Hell, I'm not going to work today, or the day after that."

Those were the words locked into her mind, and then the words became her actions. In her eyes Karter became an automated teller machine. "Babe, can I have some more money!" she asked.

"All right." He was dishing out crazy currency, and paying the household bills. Karter was madly in love with Nikki. He was a good man, so it was *automatic for him to provide her with the best. He wanted to take good care of his darlin Nikki.* Her sex was good, and it rocked his world. Her vagina was warm like the sun. After getting some, he felt like shining, and strove to be the best man he could possibly be. Coincidentally, Sunshine was her nickname too. He was addicted to her love. Nikki's sex gave him everlasting energy and he felt like a brand-new man every time they had intercourse, but this woman was so slick. She used sex to her advantage, and she had Karter right where she wanted him.

Karter was watching television as she walked into the room and said, "Hey, babe!"

"How was your day?" he asked.

Nikki walked over to him, and gave him a kiss. "It was good."

She had two huge designer bags with outfits in them. She loved Gucci, Prada, Louis Vuitton, Dolce, Tommy Hilfiger, and Gabbana.

"I see you went shopping again." Karter looked hot.

"Yeah! I'm a woman and that's what we do," she said jokingly. Nikki knew how to smooth things over. She started massaging his shoulders to relieve the tension in his body. She slipped him a deep French kiss.

Dazzled by her kiss, all he could say was, "Oh. Okay!"

In her closet hung every kind of designer label, some with the price tags still attached. Their relationship had taken a dead-end turn to the wrong destination. The love in which had come on so strongly in the beginning of their relationship was now only a controlling factor in their relationship. Karter dangled like a puppet on a string. He didn't have control over himself anymore. Karter hated the feeling of being taken advantage of. His scorned heart was filled with pain. His soul was numb. He contemplated and contemplated, thinking back to a time when their relationship had been so good. Karter eventually got tired of feeling like shit, so he decided to confront Nikki about it. An image of her when they first met flashed before him. Her pretty big blue eyes staring directly up at him.

"Sunshine, *why you want to treat me so bad*? When you know that I love you!"

"I love you too baby!"

"No, you don't love me anymore!"

She looked at him, perplexed. "Why would you say a silly thing like that?"

"It is not silly!"

"Honey, of course I still do love you... I do!"

Karter's heart hurt deeply. "Sunshine, I can't make you love me if you don't. I can't make your heart feel something it won't. Honestly, it feels like it's only about money with you. Actions speak volumes, louder than words. The super nice things you use to do for me you don't do anymore. When I'm at work *how come you don't call me anymore* just to see how my day is going?"

Nikki just sat there listening without responding.

"The love-making is good, but I don't want our relationship to be strictly based on sex. I want a metaphysical relationship!"

She gave him a confused look. "Karter, what are you talking about?"

"Sunshine, it's a relationship of the mind. Because a relationship without the mind will never last forever." Karter shook his head. "Baby, I could feel you slipping away from me. Why don't you surprise me like you use to anymore?"

Nikki looked startled. "Huh, what?"

Karter looked at her seriously. "You used to cook lasagna, my favorite. Do you remember?"

Nikki tried to play it off. "Just because I don't do the things I used to do doesn't mean I don't love you anymore."

"Okay, so what does it mean?"

She avoided the question, diverting back and answering his previous question. "Yes, Karter! I remember cooking you lasagna."

Karter stared at her in dismay. "Sunshine, I want to feel appreciated by you! Damn it, stop taking me for granted. At the beginning of our relationship you were super thoughtful, and you did a lot of nice things unexpectedly. These days it seems the only thing you are good for is asking for this and that. Well you make love to me good too, but I need more than just sex from you!"

*Money didn't matter.* It was about his love for Nikki. Karter wanted to provide her with the finer things in life, but at the same time he wanted to be loved, respected, and appreciated in return. The rejection he kept bottled inside from football spiraled out of control. He picked up a photo of them together that was sitting on the table and threw it to the ground. The frame shattered into several pieces.

"Damn you and this kooky love affair!" His voiced rose "Do you hear me, Sunshine? Can you understand what the hell I'm telling you?"

With a blank stare in her eyes, it seemed as though her head were underwater.

"Can you hear me, Sunshine?"

"Babe, I am so sorry you feel this way!" she finally said. "It hurts me to hear you talk nonsense. I still love you, and with all of my heart... you already know that, though! I promise to do better, and I will prove my love to you." She followed her words with a soft tender *kiss*. Nikki was running her game on Karter all over again. He was being pulled right back into her web of love. He's spinning, and spinning around. He was so caught up he couldn't escape Nikki's love. After a few months of being on her best behavior, their relationship went right back to the same pattern.

*Sometimes it snows in April, and people can make you feel so bad.* Karter felt incomplete, and confused inside his heart about Nikki's *l*ove. *On* a dark, cold, and lonely evening, the lights were slightly dimmed to increase a romantic mood. Red and pink rose petals outlined a heart shape on the shiny waxed hardwood floor.

The smell of aromatherapy oils and candles circulated around the room. A bottle of Chardonnay along with two champagne glasses were sitting on the nightstand.

Nikki lay in the bed, wearing beautiful red and white iridescent lingerie from Victoria's Secret. Her hair was pinned up messy, but looked so pretty. She motioned with her pointer finger to Karter. "Come over here, honey! I have a present for you," she said in a very scandalous, seductive tone.

He chuckled and walked closer to Nikki. "What kind of

present do you have for me, baby?" Kissing her lips, and softly stroking her body, he sucked on her neck like it was a sweet strawberry. "You look so damn sexy! *Let's pretend we're married* and go all night. Just *do me baby like you* never done before," he whispered in her ear.

Nikki smiled. When it came to sweet love-making Karter was not a one-minute man. *Slow love* he took his time satisfying her until her body got enough of him. His muscular body went up and down and around and around like the horses on a merry go round, as he slowly and deeply penetrated her vagina. Karter worked up a *black sweat*, hitting every spot to make her scream. Nikki started yelling out his name. "Karter! Karter! Karter! I'm going to cum!" The love juices flowed, as she finally *creamed*.

They relaxed in each other's arms. Karter presumed Nikki was floating in the clouds too, because of feeling properly loved by a man who was truly infatuated by her, but her feelings were not in it anymore.

After making passionate love to Nikki, he held her closely. The tingling of sweet love adorned his heart, overflowingly, but the feelings were not totally mutual. With her it was only about a sexual feeling. Love had left her heart a long time ago. So, there was no longer a deep emotional connection.

She kept dishing out more and more lies of betrayal. She was only selfishly concerned about herself, and what she could get out of their relationship. Nikki was willing to give just a little bit of effort to persuade Karter that she was madly in love with him a hundred percent. She was blessed with the give of gab, and knew how to work the bullshit quite advantageously. Nikki could win an Oscar for best actress, because acting was exactly what she was doing.

"Sunshine, so how was your day?"

"Babe, it was an all right kind of day. But guess what, handsome? The night is young and being here with you makes me feel jovial. Spending quality time with you is more fulfilling than anything in this world! You holding me in your arms is priceless, honey. Every time I am with you, I feel like a princess!"

*He* kissed her. "You are my beautiful princess!" Karter was slowly falling for the lies again.

After taking a relaxing hot, steamy bubble bath, she slipped into a black silk robe. Nikki made her way back to the bedroom. She dropped her robe to the floor, and his eyes bulged as he admired her sensuous body. Nikki's breasts were double d's, firm and perky.

"Baby, I love you!" she said. Karter grabbed a bottle of Johnson and Johnson baby oil. He started massaging and oiling her from head to toe. Nikki slyly smiled. "Babe, I went shopping today at the Galleria Mall. I saw a bad ass one-piece jumpsuit. It was black suede with gold glitter. It looked really gorgeous on me, too! It was something kind of special. I know you would love to see me in it, wouldn't you?"

Karter stared at her still with the look of love in his eyes.

"Heck, yeah," he replied. "Really, you fancy it?"

"I like it, all right."

"Okay, I'll give you some money later. But right now, what I need from you is another round of some sweet love making, baby. Come here with your sexy ass and give me some sugar!" Their lips locked and the passion sparks flew, but of course, the emotions only grew stronger for Karter. Karter and Nikki's relationship seem to be headed in the right direction, at least he assumed so, but after a long, exhausting day at work he was ready to get home so he could relax with his Sunshine. As soon as he opened the door, he heard the *screams of passion. It sounded like love-making.* Then, he realized the moans and groans were coming from the upstairs bedroom. Once he made it up, he rushed straight into the room. There she was, his Sunshine lying in the bed, naked and covered in baby oil. She had been watching the television with the volume turned up to the maximum. A hot steamy provocative pornographic flick was playing on the T.V. screen. Karter's eyes suspiciously wandered around the bedroom. Nikki was so antsy, but of course she played it off really well. "Hello, baby! How was your day?"

She quickly ran up to him, kissing his lips and touching his love muscle, caressing his body all over, hoping her distractions would *get him off the subject*. While he was being distracted, Nikki's other man silently crept right out of the side door.

Karter slipped Nikki a beautifully-wrapped gift. The card read, 'I love you' all over it, and in red, white, and black. He was so excited to give her the gift. "This is for you!"

"Thank you, honey!" Anxiously, Nikki grabbed and opened it.

"How are you, baby?" Karter said.

"My day is much better now!" It was the bad-ass one-piece black suede gold glitter jumpsuit she had desired by Tommy Hilfiger, and a *diamond and pearls* necklace. "Aw, this is so gorgeous babe! I love it and you too!" She tightly squeezed him as they hugged and tongued each other down.

Nikki was a despicable yet clever woman. It was as if she had attended a course on Slickology 101, because in any and every situation, she always knew how to wiggle herself right out of it. Without a doubt she was very dangerous and because Karter loved her so much, he chose to ignore all the warning signs. He was oblivious to the lies and her cheating. Lie after lie came out of her venomous mouth. Being deceptive was what she knew how to do best. Of course, he was not totally elated with their relationship, but because he invested everything into their three-year relationship, he just could not walk away. Karter couldn't throw in the towel like football.

The road became even more rough. Karter's job was planning layoffs. Funds became scarce, and they could not spend frivolously. Nikki's shopping sprees were limited, and eventually ceased altogether. At first she agreed to it. Then she went right back to her old habitual ways. Nikki constantly shopped, and over a six-month period, the balance at Wells Fargo was zero. The signs of her love and affection diminished too. The *thief of the temple* took Sunshine's love away from Karter. He noticed the sudden change in her behavior. Nikki was a totally different woman than she was before, especially, from the beginning of their relationship. Once the cash had gone away, she slipped away. She started staying out a little later, and lying even more.

It was midnight, and Karter's heart was lonely. His body badly hot and horny. Thoughts of Nikki always gave him a *dirty mind*. When he fell asleep, he dreamed of her.

She walked into the house and snuck into the bedroom. After putting on her jogging pants and a t-shirt, Nikki slipped into the bed. Karter was sound asleep, but he was awakened by the motion of the waterbed.

Rolling over, he softly tapped her leg.

Nikki rolled over to face him, and kindly said the words that every man dreaded hearing. "I am on my period! Sorry, babe, we can't have sex tonight." She said it with such pleasure.

"What, really?" A lot of women used this tactic. Especially when they are not in the mood to make love or have sex. It was called *pussy control*. Karter wanted to make love to her so badly. "Damn it!" he sighed.

She rolled over and fell fast asleep. He could not help but reflect back on how their relationship used to be. Especially in the love and romance department. He asked the question to himself. "Why are things so different between us?" He could not understand why their love was shifting into a different direction. They were drifting further and further apart. After much contemplating, he knew what he needed to do. He had to confront Nikki about it again. Karter desperately tried to hang onto what he wanted to convince himself was a healthy relationship, but it was definitely not a good one.

Saturday night, Karter rested in the bed with financial worries on his mind. He lay in total humiliation, as the car tires traveled over the wet, rain-soaked roads outside. He felt the pain being lonely could bring. He could not help but feel neglected and unloved. Karter quickly jumped up and took a look into the closet.

Seeing every garment of Nikki's had vanished, he dashed to the bedroom window. Her car was not parked outside. No car and sign of her anywhere. He patiently waited for her to return home. The next day came and went. It was an overcast Sunday without any sunshine in sight, she did not come home. The next day came and gone. No news about Nikki or a phone call. He sat in his lonely room looking for his Sunshine. *Seventeen days* turned into several months. *Seven*, to be exact. By this point he knew her love had disintegrated and she was never coming back to him. The money was gone, and so was her love. Every day pressing forward became a huge struggle for Karter. He questioned himself over and over again. Did she ever love me? How did this happen? Why did it happen? He could come up with only one conclusion. Karter truly loved Nikki. Every day he fantasized about her; without her love he was now lost. But they say a person's action speaks louder than words. What did Nikki's actions speak? Obviously, she only proved she was about one thing. Money!

# Sign of the Times

When it rains it pours. The economy was shitty again. People were unable to spend money as they were accustomed to doing. The situation had taken a turn for the worst, the domino effect as companies closed their doors one by one, feeling the wrath of the storm. In the aftermath, people lost their jobs. The year was 2009. Circuit City had been around for sixty years, and then they went out of business. The automobile industry took a beating too. General, Chrysler, Ford Motors, and many other companies laid off hundreds of their employees. The second time catastrophe was caused by the son of Bush, George W. Bush Jr. Coincidental, right? People slaved relentlessly their whole entire lives only to lose their houses, automobiles, stock investments and retirements.

Everything once valuable was now lost and gone.

The storm rained on Karter too. Harder than ever before, and like a thief in the night the recession stole his dignity and pride away from him. Home became the back seat of his green Ford SUV. How had Karter arrived in this horrific place? It was cold, dark, and lonely. The worst part of it was carrying a desolate degrading feeling inside of him. Life should not have turned out this way. He worked too hard for this to occur.

The number of people residing in campers and other vehicles had surged 46 percent over the past year. The problem exploded in cities with expensive housing markets, including Los Angeles, Portland and San Francisco. The problem was national in scope, although its impact was more acutely felt in urban areas. Challenges abounded for people who lived in their vehicles, ranging from parking tickets to finding a safe place to park and shower.

Karter did take accountability for his misfortune, but with the recession and layoffs happening it was totally out of his control.

How could he get a job if companies were not hiring anymore? He was at the lowest point of his life. He felt low and like he was sinking lower into life's quicksand. He even disassociated himself from Flip and Tiff. He didn't want them to see their brother as a complete failure. Tiffany had moved to Atlanta after she graduated from high school to start a new life, and Flip was able to land a career in television. They were doing pretty well for themselves.

He became antisocial and withdrawn from the world. He avoided conversations with his friends. Can you blame him? He was totally embarrassed about the outcome of his life. He did not have an appetite for food. His body had started to look a little frail, and he had a loss of energy. Day after day, and night after night the agonizing feeling of being unable to stretch out in the comforts of a nice plush bed started to take a toll on his overstressed body. Often he awoke in the early mornings with severe headaches, backaches, and a growling stomach. A lot of times he ate whatever he could get, and whatever was cheap.

He stared at a Jack-in-the-Box menu board. His hair was uncombed, and his breath unpleasant.

"Hi, can I take your order, please?" Anita said.

"Give me just a minute," Karter said. He dug deep into his right pocket and pulled out four quarters and seven cents. "Uh... can I get two tacos?" He handed her the money. His hands were cold and quivering.

"Okay. Thank you, sir."

Usually, he would order two tacos or a big deal. Yes, it was a big deal! Because his diet was no longer nutritious, his health had become troubled. Eating a lot of food high in sodium had given him high blood pressure.

All of a sudden, he began to feel faint. He felt like he was spinning. He felt dizzy. Karter staggered into the restroom to get a cold wet paper towel so he could wash his face. "Dear God, please make my head stop hurting! Sheesh! I am spinning around in circles."

When his nose started to bleed, he became frightened. Karter knew it had to be a very serious condition. "Oh my gosh! What's going on with me?" he asked himself. After finishing his cleanup, he stumbled back to the register so he could pick up his order.

"Sir, are you okay?" a customer asked.

"Yeah, I will be fine, thank you."

"Number 21," Anita shouted, grabbing his food. Suddenly, Karter had a flashback. He could see a vision of himself passing a football. He heard people screaming his name.

"Karter, Karter, Karter." Then he heard the voice of an angry fan saying, "Don't let us down!" He quickly lurched his way out of Jack in the Box.

Since Karter became unemployed, he'd lost his medical coverage, so he was unable to see a physician. The thought of going to a county hospital and having to wait in ridiculously long lines for an extremely long amount of time sickened him even more. He found quick remedies to ease his pains. His self-esteem bruised, and suffered due to the position of his circumstances.

The basic necessities of life were stripped away. Karter was unable to brush his teeth or bathe daily. When he wanted to, he had to go to a fast food restaurant like Jack in the Box or Burger King. Living life under these kinds of conditions made him feel like a bum, feeling absolutely worthless inside of his soul. Karter's so-called friends were way too busy and wrapped up into their own lives to even help him out. Friends who he thought would have his back and be in his corner had slowly turned their backs on him. They acted as if they didn't even know him anymore. It tore him up inside, thinking about how everyone smiled in his face when everything was good, and he was considered "the man." Since the tables had turned, they ran and abandoned him.

Karter did have an old friend to come to his rescue. Her name was Queenie.

"I thought they would have had my back." Karter said to her.

Although they had lost contact for some time, they were able to reconnect through social media. Queenie did not have any idea what her good friend had been going through. Coincidentally, she was going through it too. "Hello, TQ! How are you doing?"

"Queenie, not so good, but I'm hanging in there! All the time, it feels like I'm spinning. I don't know if I'm coming or going."

"TQ, how is your diet?" she asked.

"Not good."

"So, then what do you expect?" Queenie was a realist, but she didn't have the slightest clue that life was treating Karter so badly. "TQ, you have to take better care of yourself!"

"Yeah, I know," he said.

"To me it sounds like you may have high blood pressure."

"Queenie, you really think so?"

"Check it out with your doctor."

Karter was embarrassed to tell Queenie that he didn't have a doctor anymore.

"What you can do for now is get a water bottle. Fill it up with water. Add vinegar, garlic, and light honey. Then shake it up well. This simple remedy will pull your blood pressure down. But you must get to a doctor!"

"Okay. I appreciate it!" he said.

"I hope you feel better."

"Yeah, me too," he said. "Thanks, Queenie! I have to constantly turn the car heater on and off. It's really cold out here tonight. I hope I don't catch pneumonia." He started to feel sorry for himself.

"What the hell? Oh, my gosh, TQ? Are you homeless?"

Karter, ashamed, said, "Yes, I lost my job some months ago."

"Really? I lost my job too." Queenie started laughing. "These days times are so hard! I'll see what I can do. I will send you a care package. What necessities do you need?"

Karter was hesitant, and then he responded. "I could use some toothpaste, deodorant, and blankets."

"Okay, and what about food?"

"Oh, yeah! Duh, I can't survive off that alone."

Queen laughed again. "You won't last too long! How about Vitamin Water?"

"Lots of it... I have to keep my energy up. Oh, and some Cup of Noodles Soup so I can stay warm."

Queenie was puzzled. "So, how are you going to warm it?"

"I will go to 7-Eleven or something."

"Oh, okay. Can you think of anything else you would like or need?"

"Anything nonperishable is fine... oh, and some honey buns." His voice now gave off a smile. Karter felt happier, knowing Queenie had his back.

"Okay, you got it, friend!"

"Thanks, Queenie. You are the best!"

Queenie packed up the supplies and called the nearest FedEx to ship them off. It brought her to tears knowing her friend was homeless. And he had so much talent and potential. At times, the feeling of giving up on life dwelled within Karter. Karter had been unemployed for two and a half years. Because he was out of work for so long, most employers felt he was unemployable. He became so intimidated trying to find employment. Here we go again, he thought.

The second time around, and again no one would give him a job. It wasn't Karter's fault the recession occurred. It was not like he was avoiding work. He very much wanted to work and have a purpose. The mess of the recession was totally out of his control, and Karter had suffered the consequences. While applying for more positions, he kept receiving more and more rejection.

"I am here for the position."

"Sorry, the position has been filled!"

He kept knocking and knocking. "Are you hiring?"

"Yeah, but you are overqualified."

"Yesterday, I sent my resume and I am just inquiring."

"Sorry, you don't have enough experience."

Everywhere he went it was some negative bullshit. "Fuck!" Karter said. He was so sick and tired of looking for a job. He was a little older but wiser, and yet right back in the same situation. Unemployed!

What made it even worst this time around was being homeless. Thoughts of defeat constantly sucker-punched him, but he kept fighting back and searching. He desperately wanted to hear the answer "Yes!" But instead he became exhausted from hearing the word "No!" Life threw him every kind of curve ball, and he kept striking out. Karter became fed up with people and the world. But he never gave up. He kept thinking of a way to excel, to make it to the top of the ladder. He finally came up with a brilliant idea to finally put himself back on the right track. It was the best decision ever; a blue-collar career.

"Hello, trucking," Karter said to himself, keeping a positive outlook so he could move forward in his life. In order for him to start a new career, he had to mentally motivate himself. Then, physically. He learned how to operate a trailer. He finished trucking school and received his CDL license.

After a few months of regaining his confidence, Karter had a newfound profession. He was finally ready to utilize his new skills in the world.

He was making money in a whole new, unexpected career. Of course, he was over the moon about his newfound occupation, but after a few months of working, there were a few confrontations. Some of the other truckers felt he did not belong in the company. Because of his eloquent grammar and higher education, he was out of place. It was clearly visible. Here was a highly educated and intelligent man, working as a truck driver.

Karter walked inside the joint, bubbly. The evil eye of a trucker stared directly at him. "Good Morning," Karter said.

"Hey, boy! What the hell are you doing here?" Doug asked.

Karter tried to remain calm. "Trying to make a living just like you. Look here, you don't have to like me, and I don't have to like you either. But we need to respect each other!"

"I don't have to respect your ass! You fucking want to be white boy! I bet you think you're better than the rest of us."

"Huh?"

"Just because you have a little education, and a degree under your belt? You think you all high and mighty, huh?"

"What?" Karter said. "Man, look here. You don't want no smoke. I have a job to do, and not you or anybody else in this world is going to stop me. So leave me the hell alone." Karter pushed open the front door of the company. "Man, stay the fuck out of my way," he said.

When he made it to his truck one of the tires was flat.

"Ain't this about a bitch!" He said to himself. These were the types of issues Karter dealt with, especially once he graduated from college. He always was an easy target because of how he articulated his words and carried himself. To blacks he was not black enough, and to whites he was trying to be "too white."

This time around Karter made a decision. He wasn't going to let anyone or anything intimidate him. In life, you had to do what's right for you, and what makes you smile. He was finally happy and at peace with himself. Karter stood his ground, and fought hard for his respect. Facing his fears, he wasn't going to run away and hide. He stood strong and proud, driving from sunny Southern California as far as the Big Apple. Cruising whether it was raining, snowing or the sun was shining. Karter picked up the company's loads one after another and made the drops. He was finally able to live life feeling good about himself, being free, and not feeling like a prisoner of society. Karter felt validation for his achievements.

Working in the corporate world, Karter had always felt like he was walking on pins and needles, feeling uncomfortable every second, but as a trucker he felt more at ease. There was nothing more gratifying than knowing you can set a goal and conquer it.

# Karma is a Bitch

Karter was awakened out of a deep sleep by three rings of the telephone. "Hello, who dis?"

Nikki was quiet for a second. Suddenly a high-pitched cry projected through the line. "Hello, this is Nikki!"

Karter's heart started beating faster. Whenever he heard her voice, it gave him uncontrollable butterflies. He looked down and noticed his left hand shivering. His nerves were tweaking. Ms. Conniving Nikki had a strong effect on him. She had total control over him, but how could he be so naïve? Karter knew he had to stand his ground, and let her know he wasn't a wimp ass, but a man who was in control of himself and his destiny. Karter couldn't forget that Nikki had up and left him, obviously saying, "To hell with you!" He was feeling flustered again as he remembered how she abandoned him, seven-and-a-half months ago. With every ounce of his heart aching, he asked, "What the hell do you want? Never mind. I'm about to hang up!"

Nikki sniffled. "No, no wait! We need to talk!"

"Sunshine, we have nothing to talk about!" he said as his voice rose. "You left me. You can't bail out of the relationship whenever the going gets tough. Sheesh! Your communication skills though." He let out a chortle.

"I know, and I want to apologize to you for it. I'm sorry, Karter!"

Karter sat on the other end of the telephone line, confused. He could not understand how Nikki could come back after being away so long. "So, I'm supposed to act as if you never fucking left me, right? Girl, you really hurt me, and I know the reason you left, too."

"So why did I leave you, Karter?" she asked suspiciously.

"You left me because my money was depleted, and because you are a damn hungry-ass gold digger!"

"No, I beg to differ! That' not the reason I left you! Oh, and I am not a hungry-ass gold digger!"

Karter snapped angrily, "Bullshit! So why did you leave me?"

"I don't know how to tell you this."

"Tell me what, Sunshine? Just spit it out!" Karter said. "You are crazy as hell! Nikki, you're the one who broke my heart, and I am supposed to have some kind of sympathy for you?" Karter shook his head. "No, it doesn't work that way, sweetheart! I hate you! You low down dirty-ass bitch!"

"Bitch!" she repeated, shocked.

Karter just stared at the telephone with contempt. "Yes, you're a bitch! That is exactly what you are, and it was silly of me to think you really loved me! I guess it was all a front. And I had big plans for us. I wanted to marry your no-good gold-digging ratchet-ass! Do you know? *I would die for you?*"

"Stop it, Karter and wait a minute! I still do love you! Please, just listen to me for a minute."

"*Damn you!*" Karter replied. "Okay, speak your mind."

"When we were together, mentally I had a lot going on. I tried to accept the fact we were an interracial couple. I played it off as if it was not bothering me, but the people with their stares and questionable judgments... honestly, to tell you the truth my parents would never approve and accept you!"

Karter was furious. "What the hell are you talking about? After several years into our relationship, and now you finally decide you want to come clean and be honest with me." He laughed with sarcasm. "It is all starting to make sense to me now. So, is that the reason you never wanted to take me to meet your folks, because you were ashamed of my skin color?"

Nikki sat quiet, listening to Karter.

"Wow! God created people to be people. I want to read a poem to you!" He recited a poem by one of his favorite authors, Yetta Yvette. "It's called *Love is Love*! Love has no boundaries, love is unconditional, love doesn't discriminate or eliminate, when you truly love someone. It's not about age, race, or creed; love is about two people with strong feelings who need each other to survive. Love tells no lies; when you know it is true, love makes you a better you," he finished. "Because of you I'm a better man! That's what you have done for me. Can you comprehend it, Sunshine? Obviously, you can't see it. I know our relationship is one-sided. You don't feel the same way I do."

"But I do Karter!"

Karter shouted out through the telephone, "Love is color blind!"

He could not see Nikki's expressions, but imagined her eyes were filled with tears. "Yeah, Karter! I know, but my parents are old-fashioned, and they have their beliefs. Why do you think I was always so secretive when it came time for you to meet them? Why do you think I changed the subject every time? My mother and father are from the old school. They would never understand or accept our relationship."

"What the hell, Sunshine? Wow, really?" he asked. "You could have told me. I would have understood!" Karter was so livid his voice became shaky. He finally broke down. This was a very sensitive emotional side of him that Nikki had not witnessed before. Not knowing what to say, Nikki was hesitant to respond.

Karter took a deep breath. "Sunshine, we were supposed to be in love! It is not about your parents. It should have been about you and me!"

"I know, but at the time I never wanted to feel like I had to choose between you and my family. I know how I feel. I know what I want, and that is you!"

Karter laughed. "Are you serious? It took you seven and half months to realize how you felt about me."

"Karter, I need to see you in person, so, we can talk face to face and discuss our relationship a little more in-depth. I know you still love me, honey, because I will always have love inside my heart for you," she said.

Karter thought his ears was deceiving him, so he hesitated. "Why?" Karter asked. "What difference does it make if we see each other face to face? If I see you, I don't know how I will react. I might have a flashback of the pain, and Sunshine, I don't want to hurt you!"

"C'mon babe, please!" Nikki begged. "C'mon, pretty please with a cherry on top!"

Karter became aggravated by her persistence. "Why, Nikki?" Karter pretended he did not want to see Nikki, but deep down inside his heart he really did. He was playing the hard to get role, trying to make her believe he was such a tough cookie, when actually he was as soft as a roll of Charmin toilet paper. "Okay! Okay! Okay!" he said, giving in.

"Okay, can you meet me at the Starbucks on **A**l*phabet Street a*t three o'clock?" Nikki asked.

"A'aight, I will be there and you better not be late because I will leave."

"Karter, no! I will be there and on time!" There was a smile in her voice. Nikki knew she was an *irresistible bitch,* and that Karter was so weak for her. "All right, I will see you then."

"Okay, bye," Karter said. After hanging up the telephone, Karter couldn't believe Nikki was able to persuade him to meet her, but he always had a weakness for her, and a weird sensation inside in his heart. Love can make you do some crazy-ass things.

It was hot and humid, and the time was 2:45 p.m. Nikki

pulled up in an older model *little red corvette*. She arrived approximately fifteen minutes early, parked, and waited. It was three o'clock exactly when Karter pulled up in his green SUV. There she was, sitting in her car, and sipping on a matcha green tea smoothie. He parked his car and noticed *Ms. hot thing* near a shade tree. He walked over to her vehicle.

Karter was still baffled by the reason they had to meet. "Hey, so what's up Sunshine?"

When Nikki got out of her car, she reached over to give him a hug, her belly stuck out. "Wow, what the hell, so you are pregnant? Is it mine?" Karter asked. He did the mathematics in his head, thinking that the kid could be his. "Is that what this is about?"

Nikki sighed. Karter stared at her stomach.

"Damn, girl you are humongous!" He smiled at her. "I want the truth out of you, Sunshine. I am asking you again... is it mine? You better not lie to me this time!" He gave her a hard look; he wasn't bullshitting. "Don't you lie to me. Damn, why is it so hard for you to just tell me the truth? Damn!"

"Okay, okay, okay... No, it is not your baby."

Karter shook his head. "Sunshine, for once in your damn life you told me the truth." Karter laughed. "So, why am I here?"

"I really miss you Karter!" She reached her arms out to him.

Karter pushed her hands away from him. "Well, *I hate you!*"

She kept moving in closer to him. "No, don't say that, babe! I was hoping you could somehow forgive me for the past. I still love you, and I want you back!"

"Are you fucking kidding me? You could not possibly be serious! So, where is your baby's daddy?"

Nikki's face turned scarlet. "I am embarrassed to tell

you, but he left me." A tear rolled down her cheek.

Karter wanted Nikki to hurt like he was hurting. "You see what happens when you deal with a man who you think you know, but you really don't know shit about. He probably was a one-night stand too, huh?"

"No, he was not a one-night stand," she said sarcastically, ashamed.

Of course, he had to rub it in. "When you had a good man, you didn't want me! Sunshine, you didn't seem to be the kind of woman who was superficial or shallow, but only money matters to you."

"No, that's not true! I do love you!" she said. "We can start over again, and this time I promise everything will be good! Karter, I promise!"

He gave her a disbelieving look. Karter couldn't believe what he was listening to. He became upset with Nikki because it was like she was insulting his intelligence. "Do I look like a damn idiot or something? You want me to be Captain save-a-ho, right? Because that is exactly what you are- a ho! How are you going to get pregnant by another man when you claim to love me? You are so trifling. Shit!"

"No, I really do love you!" Nikki's voice cracked. "Do you still love me? I know you have to still care or else you would not have met me today."

Karter stared at her. "Honestly, Sunshine, yeah, I do care. Maybe even love you a little bit still. Because love does not disappear or go away like that," he snapped his fingers. "It can linger on in your heart forever. But after the betrayal, lies, and the hurt you put me through, I will never be able to trust you ever again. I can't get over this despair. The *condition of my heart* is fragile, and now it's broken. Now you are pregnant." Karter sat in thought for a moment. "Hell no... I can happily say it's over, baby! I'm going my way, and I suggest you go yours. *Because I could never take the place of your man.* Although I do wish you well, and your baby, too. No hard feelings. *I wish you heaven.*"

Walking away from Nikki, he threw up the peace sign. "*Deuces! Baby, I'm a star* and now your star is gone!"

She could do nothing but cry. The tears flowed down her face. She knew at once Karter was out of her life for good. He was definitely a good man, and no other man would be able to compare to him. At the time Nikki hadn't realized it, but Karter was completely gone out of her life.

Walking back to his car, he was dumbfounded. His heart yearned for her love, but his mind knew it wasn't right. As he drove home, out of nowhere it started raining massive purple raindrops. He felt blue inside. In his future he saw better days, but at the present time he was hurting deeply. Karma is a bitch! You can't mistreat a good person and think you're going to prosper. Just when you think you can, it'll come back around and bite you in your ass every time! And like the old saying, "You never miss a good thing until it is gone," Karter was gone for good.

Karter knew that the sad thing about it was the next woman who came along could be "the one," but he probably wouldn't be so nice because of his fear of being hurt and rejected again. When it came to love, you had to be able to start anew, a fresh clean slate, and let your guard down a little, because every woman and man were not the same.

# As the World Turns

Queenie was going through it too. She was dealing with love's ups and downs. She was so exhausted from getting her feelings hurt over and over again. Eventually, she made up her mind she was going to wait for the real deal. On this one particular night the sky looked so surreal. It was looking some kind of beautiful. The glow of the night was astonishing. Queenie had never seen it look like this before. The stars were glistening very brightly, in the midnight darkness.

"Twinkle, twinkle, little star," she said, "who is the fairest of them all?"

Looking deeper into the sky, she wondered when true love would ever find her. It was every woman's fantasy. Queenie desired to be madly in love with a man who was not afraid to expose his true feelings. Not just by confessing his love by saying the words, "I love you!" His actions had to signify and match it too.

Shawn and Queen watched a good movie and then an argument began. After the arguing subsided, they walked in utter silence from the movie theater. While walking to the car Queenie's thoughts got the best of her. "You really just don't get it, do you?" she asked. "We have problems in our relationship only because you don't understand me as a woman."

Shawn looked into Queenie's pretty dark brown eyes. His look indicated he thought she was speaking nonsense. "What are you talking about?" He started mimicking her, hoping it would make her shut up. "Queenie, get inside the car!"

Shawn walked over to the passenger's side of the car and opened his door.

Queenie was pissed. "Shawn, you're supposed to open a lady's car door first. A gentleman opens the car door for a woman. Not to mention, you should be driving in the first damn place anyways!" Queenie was so annoyed with Shawn's behavior.

He started mimicking her again.

"Wow, Shawn you really are childish! Man, you have a lot of growing up to do."

When Queenie said the word childish, it struck a nerve. The bell rang, and it was round one.

Queenie and Shawn were bouncing up and down making their way into the middle of the ring. There was no referee in a black and white striped shirt. The gloves were on, and the humiliating insults were being tossed back and forth. The words were so disparaging. A punch straight to the heart.

"Ouch! Damn, it hurts!" Her soul felt wounded. She swerved to avoid a big pothole. Out of nowhere came flashing lights.

"Damn it!" Queenie yelled. The sound of a police siren approached. When she looked into her hazy rearview mirror, she was blinded by the lights. Her eyes became irritated.

A baritone voice ejected from the squad car. "Pull over to the right!"

She was not anticipating trouble because she was not riding dirty. Queenie's driver's license, registration, and insurance were current and up to date. "See, Shawn, look what you made me do!"

"I did not do shit!" he said, and laughed. "It's all on you driving like a crazy lady. Just pull over like the cop said."

"What could this madness be about?" Queenie wondered. She pulled over. As the officer approached, she felt nervous and afraid, especially after the recent police brutalities. "Yes, officer? What seems to be the problem?"

"Ma'am, I noticed you swerved back there on Main Street. Are you inebriated?"

"What?" Queenie was shocked. "Are you kidding me?"

"Are you intoxicated? Have you been drinking?"

She burst into helpless laughter. "No, and I'm not stupid, officer. I know what inebriated means." Her smart-ass response annoyed and angered the officer. She started laughing.

"What is so funny?" he responded.

"I can't believe you just asked me have I been drinking."

"Why are you ignoring the question?" Raising his voice, he snapped, "I asked you have you been drinking?"

"No, officer!" Queenie giggled. "My boyfriend and I just had a little argument, that is all! I want to live! People who drink and drive apparently don't." She was not trying to be sarcastic, but the officer interpreted her facetious manner that way.

"Can I see your driver's license and registration please?" Queenie looked up and gave a sneaky grin. She pulled the envelope that contained all of her information out of the glove compartment and handed it over to him.

"Miss, get out of the car!"

"Okay," She replied. As she got out of the car, she kept calm.

"So, you want to be a smart ass, huh?"

Queenie read the name on his badge. "No, not by any means Officer Keith."

"I want you to walk the line and take a breathalyzer test."

"But why?" she asked. "Okay, but like I told you before, I have not been drinking!"

Queenie was disturbed, but remained cool and relaxed. It was pretty tough under the circumstances. She walked a straight line and took the breathalyzer test. She passed it with flying colors. Officer Keith became very aggravated with her nonchalant attitude. He pulled a flashlight from his belt and shone the light directly into Queenie's eyes. "Damn, Officer Keith, what's up? I told you I haven't been drinking!"

Officer Keith slapped handcuffs around her wrists, jerking her back and forth, handling her in an extremely aggressive manner. She just stood there in agony. What had she done? Absolutely nothing! She was completely innocent.

Officer Keith opened the rear door of the squad car. "Sit your ass in the car and wait!" he said. Officer Keith stood there examining her paperwork and checking to make sure she did not have any warrants.

Queenie waited patiently in the car. "Queenie, shut up!" Shawn yelled. "Do you want to go to jail tonight? Stop having a bad attitude, and just listen to the officer!"

"No Shawn, I don't want to go to jail. But they shouldn't be harassing us for nothing! We didn't do anything wrong to deserve this kind of treatment! You know and I know that."

"But if you don't stop it, they're going to plant some shit on us! You know, some drugs. Then, we will be going to jail for sure!"

"A'aight! A'aight!" It was difficult listening to Shawn, but she did. Especially when she felt they were being harassed for no apparent reason.

Queenie was humiliated to the point of bawling. A tear ran down her face. To be accused of something you did not do is not a great feeling. The hurt kept building up inside of her.

His partner said, "C'mon, Keith. Won't you lighten up?"

The asshole of a cop snatched her purse and shook her belongings onto the hood of the squad car. Her favorite burgundy color Mac lipstick and perfume rolled off, hitting the ground and breaking. "Stop!" she said.

Queenie was humiliated. She became very upset and her cool went straight out the window. "Officer Keith, I have given you everything needed!" The hostility in her grew stronger and stronger. "I have given you my paperwork! I've proven to you I am not intoxicated! So why are you harassing us like this?"

"Shut up! I'm the one who asks the fucking questions. I'm the authority around here, I'm the one in charge!" Pointing at his chest, he said, "Do you see this motherfucking badge? You better respect it and me."

"Okay, man! That's enough!" the sidekick cop said. He had about enough of his partner's bully ass behavior. "Man, come on! Let them go! Everything appears to be good!" he shouted.

"Okay, okay..." Officer Keith said. "We're going to let you guys go with a warning this time, but stay out of trouble!"

"What trouble, Officer Keith?" Queenie asked.

Shawn quickly started coughing. "Queenie, please just be quiet! Okay, officers we sure will," he said. After being tormented for at least thirty to forty-five minutes they were finally able to go on their way. "Queenie, let's go," Shawn said. "This time I will drive."

Queenie laughed. "So, now you want to drive?"

"Yeah."

"You should have been driving in the first damn place! Let's get the hell out of here!" She said shaking her head. Queenie's mouth was always like a gun, and her slick words the ammunition. Shawn knew better not to respond or else it would have been World War III. On the drive home, Queenie thought hard.

She opened her apartment door and walked straight over to the telephone so she could call Karter. Queenie had always been there for him, and now she needed Karter to be there for her, like a good friend always does. She picked up the telephone and dialed his number.

"Hello?" Karter answered. She sniffled. "Who is this? Queenie is it you?"

She sat there silently.

"Queenie answer me! I know it's you. I can see your phone number on my caller I.D."

Queenie tried to get a grip on herself so she could speak. "Yes, it is me," she mumbled.

"Girl, what's wrong with you? Did someone hurt you? Do I need to kick somebody's ass or what? Girl, what's up? Talk to me," he said.

"TQ, I am so pissed off right now! After leaving the movie theater with Shawn, we got pulled over."

"No shit?"

"TQ, I am for real! I'm just trying to get a hold of myself."

"So what happened?"

"Shawn and I had another freaking argument. Due to the argument I swerved, and the cops thought I had been drinking. I had to walk the line, take a breathalyzer test, and everything."

"So, were you drinking?"

"Hell no!" she said. "I wasn't drinking, but they harassed us like crazy, man. Even threw my belongings on the hood of their squad car. I am so devastated and embarrassed right now. All of this occurred right in front of Shawn, too."

"Damn, really?" Karter said. "I'm so sorry you guys had to go through that shit. Dudes deal with the bullshit on an regular basis. But when a lady is involved it's not cool! I know you must be pissed."

"Hell yeah, I'm still hot. Can you see the fumes coming through the telephone?" They both laughed. Although Queenie was hurt, she still tried to have a sense of humor about the fiasco. Karter had some words of advice for her.

"Do you know what I think?"

"No, what?" she asked.

"I think you need to get rid of Shawn's sorry ass. Queenie, you deserve so much better. He's not a man. He is an asshole and a punk! Every time you guys go out on a night on the town, he angers you. What kind of relationship is that? I am just keeping it one-hundred with you, so don't get upset with me, okay?"

"Okay," she said.

"You don't deserve a man like Shawn! He does not know how to treat you like the lady you are. Maybe it's because he is egotistical. I watched him hurt your feelings time and time again. I hate to see you get hurt. What you need is a strong man, because you are a very strong woman! Not a man who does not value you."

Queenie appreciated Karter's opinion. It was the truth and she needed to hear it, instead of living in denial for the rest of her life. "I value your honesty," she said. "TQ, I know you're right. Our relationship was so good in the very beginning, but now it seems all we do is argue."

Karter just listened. He knew Queenie loved Shawn, but it was just like his romance with Nikki: one-sided. To be in a good healthy relationship takes two willing, mature people for it to work out. Karter knew the right words to say to Queenie, so it would console her because he was in the same boat. "It is going to be all right. Just give it some time. Time will heal the woe. I always got your back, right?" he asked.

"Yes, I know."

Karter could relate to her, so he was very sympathetic to her need. "I got the munchies big time. Queenie, I'm about to hit up In-N-Out and get a double-double. Do you want anything?"

She laughed. "Yeah right! Like you are about to drive my way! Nah, I am good! What state are you in now?"

"Actually, I am not too far away from you," he laughed.

"I'm in Arizona. You sure you don't want anything? I got you!"

"No thanks, TQ!" She laughed. "I appreciate you looking out for me!"

"Girl, make sure you get something to eat."

"TQ, I'm not hungry. My heart is aching. I am going to try and get some sleep."

"Okay, yeah! Don't sweat it Queenie. Sweet dreams."

"Sweet dreams, TQ.

"A'aight then. I'll catch you later."

After getting off the telephone, Queenie laid in her bed imaging what silence looks like. Staring into space, she thought of the devastating experience with the cops until she drifted off into sleep. Because of Karter's words, Queenie felt more relieved, and she was more at peace. But now her outlook on police officers would never be the same, and just because of one bad experience. Over time, maybe she would develop some resentment towards them all like Karter's experience with Julie, the hiring manager.

Eventually, Queenie left Shawn for good. His maturity level hadn't caught up quick enough to hers. Going forward, Queenie focused on self-improvement. She devoted her time to studying, working out, and getting her body into great shape. Queenie enjoyed learning and finding out about herself.

"Who am I?" she asked herself. Because she was not so focused on love, out of nowhere love hit her like a wrecking ball. Queenie fell deeply in love with a man who was not afraid to give one hundred percent of himself and his heart. She had prayed for a good man. God heard her prayers and he appeared, knocking at her door. Queenie knew deep down inside her heart she was loved by him, because her new-found love always backed his words up with actions. Mister risked everything for her, a huge sign of love. It was the assurance she needed. Her new relationship was much different from the game-playing and arguments she had dealt with from Shawn. Queenie's new relationship was entirely on a whole another level.

# Afterword

Life hasn't been the easiest. Every situation has given me a better outlook and understanding. When I reflect back on every struggle, I've grown to appreciate them because they're the great lessons learned from my experiences. It has taught me respect, strength, character, and the discipline to achieve my goals and dreams. When I thought I was losing I was in reality winning. The challenges built every fiber of my being, causing me to become who I am. Life shaped me into a masterpiece, and it wasn't until I grew older that I truly realized it.

# Bonus Material

## from the

# Author

# Football Inspirational Quotes

Some people think football is a matter of life and death. I assure you it's much more important than that.
-Bill Shanklye

The game of life is a lot like football. You have to tackle your problems block your fears and score your points when you get the opportunity.
-Louis Grizzard

Football teaches you hard work. It takes a lot of unspectacular preparation to have spectacular results in both business and football.
-Roger Staubaugh

If you believe in yourself and have dedication and pride and never quit, you'll be a winner. The price of victory is high but so are the rewards.
-Paul Bear Bryant

Without self-discipline, success is impossible, period.
-Lou Holtz

The difference between a successful person and others is not a lack of strength, not a lack of knowledge, but rather a lack of will...
-Vince Lombard

In life, as in football, you won't go far unless you know where the goalposts are.

-Arnold H. Glasgow

Football is a game about feelings and intelligence.
-Jose Mourinho

I learned that if you want to want it bad enough, no matter how bad it is you can make it.
-Gale Sayer

I believe in being driven and strong willed for success. If you get derailed in life, don't give up! Just get the hell back on the track.
-Yetta Yvette

You miss 100 percent of the shots you don't take.
-Wayne Gretzky

Good players inspire themselves; great players inspire others.
-Unknown

It's not the size of the dog in the fight, but the size of the fight in the dog.
-Archie Griffin

Today I will do what others won't so tomorrow, I can do what others can't.
-Jerry Rice

Nobody who ever gave his best regretted it.
-George Halas

Champions are willing to do what they hate; in order to get what they love.
-Unknown

Sometimes life has a way of knocking the hell out of you and killing your joy... but NEVER give up!
-Yetta Yvette

Show class, have pride, and display character. If you do wining takes care of itself.
-Paul Bear Bryant.

Build up your weakness until they become your strong points.
-Knute Rockne

Do right. Do your best. Treat others as you want to be treated.
-Lou Holt

To me, football is so much about mental toughness, its digging deep it's doing whatever you need to do to help a team win and that comes in a lot of shapes and forms.
-Tom Brady

There is always a reason for our struggles. It is God preparation for a blessing. When you feel like giving up hang in there! Because you are only a footstep away from the finish line.

Depression/Mental Illness is real! If you are having thoughts of suicide, call the **National Suicide Prevention Lifeline at: 1-800-273-8255**

Talk or go to www.SpeakingofSuicide.com for a list of additional resources.

# True Hardcore Facts

In 2008 and 2020, first a horrendous recession, and then the Corona Virus pandemic disaster hit us, bringing with it an even worse recession. More and more people have been unable to seek employment.

The percentage of people looking for work is always escalating. According to the New York Times unemployment, since May of twenty-thirteen stands out a whooping, 7.6 percent. While Black unemployment is almost doubled time higher with 13.5 percent. (According to the Bureau of Labor Statistics.) Why? Over the years, the population of people have dramatically increased. According to the Internet Consensus Report, back in the year of two-thousand was estimated that there were 281,421,906 people in the world. In 2013 the population has grown to be over 316,077,000 and steady growing. The latest reports in 2016 stands out at 324,118,787 U.S. population and 7,432,663,275 Worldwide. In the year of 2017, it stands at 7,515,284,153 up 1.11%. In 2020 currently 8 billion people in the world. (According to the Internet, Worldometer). According to Fox Five News in a more recent report of July 2019.

The number of people collecting and out of work in the state of Las Vegas is 1.9 million. Nine percent lower than twelve months ago. The numbers since the 2020 pandemic are outrageous. When I heard this information from the news reporter, I could not believe my ears. In retrospect, equals out to be too many people in the world. With more and more people, it will always be more and more competition.

Every year more and more students are graduating from colleges. To find themselves unable to locate a great paying career. Unfortunately, being stuck with a crazy ass tuition bill in the sum of a house mortgage. In most cases, will take eternity to pay it off. If he or she does not land a good paying career. There is a lot of competition and everyone is going after the, "American dream." But what does it really mean?

According to Webster's Dictionary, "the American dream" is ideal that every US. citizen should have an equal opportunity to achieve success, and prosperity through hard work, determination and initiative. I asked that question to a few chosen people, and these were the responses. "To be treated equally." "Not having to work two, and three jobs." "In order to have a decent income." Two other people said. "Having the freedom to be able to provide for my family, and have opportunities in life... To accomplish my dreams." Another said. "To own a house, cars, and have careers (or jobs that they both love). "Oh, and a pet dog." Lastly, "To retire without the headaches of not having enough money, and being able to live comfortably." Is the American dream even still obtainable in this day in age?

Indeed, I like to think so. The definition stated you must work really hard.

Nowadays in 2020 you have to have a damn good plan and strategize, because there are more and more companies going out of business or downsizing.

Businesses are always trying to eliminate, and cut the cost of expensive healthcare insurance for their employees. This is a topic in which always frustrates me. Beside the fact, when I worked for a company, I always felt I was never appreciated, and compensated for my diligence. Don't let being unable to find a job be the reason you are unable to strive, and succeed in life. Sometimes the doors will slam in your face, but one of my most favorite quotes is by Milton Berle. "If opportunity does not knock, build a door."

We have to always apply this to life's situation. When you can't find a job, then create your own job. What does it take in order for you to become successful? It takes simply four words. First, God. Secondly, good work ethics. Third, determination. Lastly, a lucky break. A lucky break is a must because it gives you a once in a lifetime opportunity. It is very essential for employers to create jobs, and give a person a chance. Even if it may mean training employees and providing job skills. Nowadays, a lot of employers don't like or appreciate doing anymore. At times, I get disappointed about life and the era we are living in compared to the past. Nowadays, more and more businesses are greedy for money, but their services are not matching up to expectation. Customer service is terrible, because most companies are not paying their employees well enough. People are working two, even three jobs, and still barely surviving. Each year inflation keeps sky rocketing, while wages level out the same.

As I watch channel thirteen news, I am in disbelief. A computerized robotic machine prepares alcoholic beverages. Then, pushes the drink forward to the customer. A lot of casinos are considering this device in order to cut out their labor force. With this kind of device, it simply replaces skilled workers. Knocking people out of bartending jobs. Inventors are creating these kinds of gadgets for the employers to cut costs. Businesses can definitely save money this way. According to an article in the Wall Street Journal it is a fact in the next ten years a lot of service jobs will be totally gone. This is horrible! Is this really our future?

Will it get any better? This is why it is very significant to focus on a career that is irreplaceable and recession proof. A career that will be around for years to come.

For example, a technician. It is about going back to school, and being trained in these kinds of fields. Eventually, robots will break down and need repairs at some point in time.

With lesser and lesser jobs, it creates more and more crimes. Another huge problem in 2020. Whenever you watch the news, you hear and see more crimes.

We are living in a time of uncertainty and struggles. Some may say we are living, in our last days. I often wonder what is going on like Marvin Gaye's 1970 song? In this era, we are still dealing with strong racism, mass massacres, police brutality, homelessness, and pure injustice. Everyday innocent people are losing their lives, because of a four-letter word, "hate." It is so devastating, when hate prevails love, when it should be reversed. Please STOP the senseless hate, and gun violence and spread LOVE!!! <3

#MyVentTime

# ADVICE

# Real Talk
*Words of Wisdom*

Over the years police brutality has escalated to its highest level. Especially for Blacks and Hispanics. Luckily for Queenie it ended well. Unfortunately, it does not always end happily. The world is going through a serious crisis. Every year going forward someone gets cut due to police brutality. Being prejudice and racist is a huge nasty sore in desperate need of antiseptic to wash away the abhorrence. So, it won't be able to continuously spread anymore. Rid the germ, so then it can heal properly. BLACK LIVES MATTER! AS WELL AS, ALL LIVES MATTER!

Rest in Power! Trayvon Martin, Michael Brown, Eric Garner, Freddie Gray, Tamir Rice, Akai Gurley, Dante Parker, Ezell Ford, John Crawford III, Tanisha Anderson, Walter Scott, Alton Sterling, Philando Castile, Dontre Hamilton, Rumain Brisbon, Jerame Reid, Tony Robinson, Phillip White, Eric Harris, Sandra Bland, Breonna Taylor, George Floyd and so many countless others who have lost their lives to police brutality.

Have you ever thought there is good, and bad in police officers? I salute those good officers who do their jobs every day, and without abusing their authority.

They put on their uniforms to a do a very dangerous job. Protecting us from the criminals of the world. They risk everything their lives and family. Sometimes losing their lives within those battles. Rodney King (RIP) said it best, the year of nineteen-ninety-two. "Can we all just get along?" For the most part when a police officer stops and pulls you over. BE COMPLIANT AND LISTEN! I know in some cases, if an officer wants to harass you, he or she will do so. But do not give them any reasons to. Will racism ever end? I don't know, but I pray it does. Rest in Peace! To anyone who have lost their lives to the hands of a police officer or vice versa. We have to choose LOVE over HATE. We need to get our acts together!

Nowadays the big problem is most folks just don't have compassion anymore!

On the roads and in life period. It sickens me. It does not matter if you are white or black. We all bleed the same red blood. If people would have the same mentality to treat each other the way they would like to be treated. This world would be a much better place!

From
# Yetta Yvette

With love why do we get caught up in appearances and perceptions? Rather than seeing the kindness of one's personality and their heart. When we first see a person who is smacking attractive we only see the outer beauty, and fall so deep in love with just that. It is an automatic and euphoric response, but what looks good on the outside is not always good on the inside. Do you remember the old saying?

Beauty is in the eyes of the beholder. When love is looking for us, we have to dig deep and not only take into consideration the flesh. For me it has always been about three attributes.

The number one attribute is the heart. To me a person with an ugly heart is indeed ugly all the way around. Number two is their intellect. How do they think?

Are they big or small minded? Can they converse on a different level that is out of this world? The next important factor is their personality. A beautiful personality is a MUST! Because no one wants to fall for an uninteresting or a boring person.

When dating most people only reveal what they want you to see and know. Over a period of time, once you get to know them better why do they change? Over time, most people will get comfortable in their relationship, and may let their guards down. When they drastically change on you or is it, they never revealed their true self to you from the jump-start? It is something to think about. This is why you have to take into consideration of being investigators when getting to know who you are dating in a relationship. What I mean by this is you have to put a person through a series of tests, so you can find out how they truly feel about you. Pay close attention to their words and actions. By doing so you won't waste a lot of time in the relationship. Especially, if it is not a good relationship. Nikki was definitely poison for Karter like the lyrics to the song Poison by Bell Biv Devoe. And that was Nikki!

Nikki released her venom attacked Karter's heart, and slowly overkilled his joy. When it comes to serious relationships love can make you so blind. Blind to what is right before your very eyes. Why do you think we sometimes settle when it comes to relationships? We settle because we want to be in love or experience it so badly. We will go to any and every measure to obtain it. We will start a relationship knowing a person is not compatible to us or they are no damn good!

And remain in a very toxic poisonous relationship only out of desperation to be LOVED! A question we have to always ask ourselves. Does my love bring me positivity or negativity? Does it cause me to want to be at my best or self-destruct? Re-evaluate! Another good question to ask yourself is do you love you?

When you love yourself, you will not tolerate bad treatment. Whether it is verbal or physical. Love should make you a better person! This is a sign you are in a healthy relationship. An important fact is you have to love and care about yourself first. Before you could truly love anyone else, and make them happy. Happiness starts within YOU! Then you take the same happiness into your relationship.

When you can see clearly through a person's bullshit smokescreen you are not subject to be played. When you are unable to see clearly you are able to be played! When you allow your feelings to make you become vulnerable this is when you can be played!

People are going to be who they are. Always remember you can never change a man or a woman to be exactly how you want them to be. Change only comes when the person is ready to change for the better and if they love you. Once you rationalize and figure it out be smart in the situation! Please don't remain captive in a relationship, and let someone abuse your heart. Because you deserve so much more than that! For God's sake, it should not be about one person expressing his or hers love more than the other. Love has to be equally balanced like a scale. Fifty/fifty nothing less and not eighty/ twenty. When two people are supposed to be in love, and the actions of one are not being reciprocated it's no good! (Meaning showing the same exact love in return.) How can we even call it love if it is not being reciprocated?

Love can be such a beautiful thing! Especially, when the feelings and actions are totally mutual. When the two hearts are on the same page with compatibility.

Most importantly be able to retain your own identity within the relationship. Two people with two hearts become one. Keep your own identity, and have your own mind! When you lose your own identity, and your own mindset in the relationship you can be led astray. Therefore, you are now under a person's control.

WARNING! Love is nothing to play with! Be extra careful! Love can hurt you to the core of your soul!

From
# Karter

During our interview Karter informed me there are strict requirements expected from the National Football League Organization (NFL). If you do not meet the criterion of their expectations a career in the NFL will not be achievable.

Depending on what position you play height and weight is extremely important!

Having early knowledge of this means every bit of difference in investing your time and energy into the sport. To me it does make a lot of sense. As a parent it is very significant not to pump a kid up with false hopes and dreams. Especially if he or she does not have the qualifications to begin with, but rather more important to persuade your child into a sports career that would be a better fit! It is more realistic!

When it comes to injury it is a football player's worst nightmare. Athletes are not invincible to them. In the early 90's Karter broke his leg. During this period of his most excruciating pain it allowed him time to digest the fact of how easily his career could have been swept away. At any given time right from under his feet. A true reality is once an athlete has an injury it is pretty terrifying. Just thinking of tweaking it all over again. Most athletes will play in fear, and play in a way of being extra careful. In order, to not reinjury their injury or injuries. This is why it is very pertinent to have a second major career to fall back on. In the case this occurs. According to Karter when choosing a career choose one based on the love of it, and not because it makes a lot of money. Your alternative career should match up with your love for the game of football, basketball, baseball etc. An error of Karter's is he chose a career in Accounting not for the love of it, but only because he wanted to put the stereotypes to rest. About athletes being dumb ass jocks. When you are passionate about your career you will challenge yourself even harder and you won't give up so easily. Why? Because you love your career.

When it comes to your own happiness in a career there is nothing to prove to people. The only person you need to prove something to is yourself! Choose wisely because if you don't you will have a lifetime to have your regrets!

Football is a very dangerous sport. Over the years there have been research and a final conclusion by Dr. Omalu Benet regarding the game of football and concussions. What is a concussion? According to the Webster's definition, a concussion is a brain injury, caused by traumatic blow to the head, or a violent shaking, of the head and body. Dr. Omalu Benet's findings were that a concussion was to blame for the erratic behavior of some football players, and many players were not even aware they even had a concussion. Which was always followed by depression and suicidal thoughts. In Karter's case, he played a quarterback position that would of or could have made him more accessible to getting a concussion. It did not occur in the game of football. Instead, it was the constant blows of his life. In which, brought on some negative behavior. There were times he would be off the chain and spiraling out of control. Depressed and other times he was just lost and confused because of the concussions of life.

# Friendship

Why do some people burn bridges? I often ask myself that question. I don't know, but God and life itself have a way of making you realize. The very same person who you thought you would never need becomes the very same person who you need the most. In life, we never know who we might need to help us out. Here is an example.

There was this guy, name Joe. He was having car problems, and he was stranded along-side the road. A man by the name of John who drives the same road seen Joe stranded with his car hood up. What did John do? Yes, he drove away without helping Joe.

Two weeks later, John was now stranded with his car hood up. Guess who was driving along? Yes, Joe. He stopped and lend John a hand. It did bother Joe because he did see John drive away and not help him when he needed his assistance. To make matters worse, they were supposed to be friends. Although John was a crummy person and did Joe wrong, Joe could not be the same kind of person. Because Joe loved to help and his heart was pure blessings flowed his way. The moral of the story is just because someone does you wrong, does not mean you have to too. We as people need to have more compassion in the world!

God is watching!

What is a good friend?

"Friends can help each other. A true friend is someone who lets you have total freedom to be yourself - and especially to feel. Or, not feel. Whatever you happen to be feeling at the moment is fine with them. That's what real love amounts to - letting a person be what he really is." - Jim

Morrison

Are you a good friend?

True Friends are rare like rainbows or a two-dollar bill. A true friend will be there for you through thick and thin. When life gets tough there are always around and never going afar. A true friend never takes the word "friendship" for granted or advantage of it. It should never be one person doing, or being a friend more than the other. Friendships should always be reciprocated. Many people boast about having a lot of friends and that is not what it is about. What is more important is who is down with you. Who has your back? A true friend is happy when you succeed in your goals and dreams. They are not waiting and hating on the sideline in hopes of your failure.

Life has its ups and downs like a scary roller coaster. Trust me I know. Life also has a way of exposing the truth. It is not about the quantity of friends, but rather the quality of friends. When you get in a bind are, they there for you? Can you ask them for a favor and without a doubt they would not hesitate? I much rather have four quarters than a whole lot of worthless pennies as friends hanging around. And that is real talk! Keep conscious and stay awake! Don't become blind to the truth of reality that is before you. Always remember in order to have a true friend you have to be a true friend!

# Words of Encouragement

A dream can become a reality, but it takes extreme motivation and dedication.

Most importantly ignoring negative people who I like to call "HATERS." Beware of a hater! A HATER is a person who hates on another person only because he or she has found their divine driven purpose. Haters hate because they desire to be where you are in life, but they are too afraid to make moves and because of their fears like a thief a hater will rob you blind of your own dream and ambition. If you decide to listen and allow them to. If someone hates on your dreams don't take it personal! Don't let them stop you, thrust forward until you are successful. One important factor to always remember is to ignore them. The acronym for "HATERS" is:

Having
Anger
Towards
Everyone
Reaching
Success

Keep in mind love overrules hate. Peace & Happiness!

I am writer who loves to write "inspire by" true events, where people were challenged and had to overcome their obstacles in life. As a non-fiction writer, I believe that books are not about their words, but rather the quality of the message that will impact the reader's life, especially when that message is based on historical lessons learned. My goal is to make you identify with my character's pain and inspire YOU!!

Football Superstar is dedicated to those who had a dream, but due to the unfortunate the dream did not manifest into reality. Being unable to conquer a goal, I know, is not a good feeling. What it can do is eat away at your heart even destroying your mind and soul. It can also cause you to become a bitter person, being ready to give up on life. Because your dream or dreams did not become in existence it does not determine you can't be victorious at another career of choice. If the plan does not work change the plan, but never the goal. It is only up to you! Do what makes you happy! Do what drive you to want to get out of bed, and start your day off with a smile! Figure it out and work effectively. It is important to be passionate about your career. Don't live your life being unhappy, feeling trap into a career that gives you no kind of gratification or self being. Even if it takes years to search and find yourself. Find out who you are! Age is nothing but a number, so step out on faith and just find you! Hustling work ethics are the components you will need before you can become successful. It is just that simple! If you are not aspiring to become at your fullest potential, don't become jealous of anyone who is. Making excuses and being cruel towards anyone who has their directional purpose is negative energy! So, why do it? When you can flip the negative energy into positive energy. Focus! #beoptimistic #workhard

# Women need Men & Men need Women

The era we live in is the norm, when young African-American boys and girls grow up without a strong presence of their fathers. Especially, for boys. Because of their absence, they will lack the love and guidance. Only a man can teach. In most case scenarios, when a young boy becomes a full, grown man and in the prime of his life, every woman he encounters will suffer. Because that very same boy who grew up without his father, exhibiting how to become a man is learning and trying to find himself as a man.

By the point of adulthood, a woman needs a man to step up, and be a man!

Most women want to be in committed relationships, and able to express their love to their men. But how can she, when she is dealing with a boy? It is not a woman's duty, or responsibility to teach a grown man. In the year of 2020, it seems the roles have reversed. Some men are taking the passenger seat, when it comes to relationships. Some men are being chauffeured by their women, and women are doing the most. In fact, their holding down careers, having children, raising them by themselves, and paying the bills in the relationship. And why? Just to be able to say, "I have a man." But I was taught, a man is supposed to show his woman how much he loves, and cares for her. He is the protector, and the provider of the family. He is the strength, and the backbone.

Being a product of a two-parent home, I witnessed a strong woman and a strong man. I am calling ALL men to rise, and step up and be a father to your children! Not just to your sons, but to your daughters too! They need you in their lives. Make a difference to the children who did not ask to come into this world, but because you birth them into the world!

Every man or woman is different. Men and women have more than just an outside surface. Like a car, there is more than just the body. Both genders have a heart, mind, and a soul. When we start to generalize, we make mistakes. Thinking every man or woman is the same, as our past relationships. It is up to you to dig deep! Find out more about the man or woman you claim to love. Get to know him or her on an interpersonal level. Which means mentally, emotionally, spiritually, and sexually. Most times, we will have only two out of the four. But when you can achieve all four, you will have a very strong connection and relationship. The worst thing you can do is make comparisons to your past relationships! You must be able to identify. If your current relationship he or she is the real deal (genuine) or superficial. Before you give mentally, emotionally, spiritually, and sexually.

Women and men need the basic necessities of life. Water, food, shelter, clothes, and LOVE! Yes, LOVE! Both genders need to have and be loved.

When it comes to love, some men and women have misconceptions. In order, to fulfill love you must have a strong understanding of the meaning. Most men and women can become so quick, and easy to say the words, "I love you!" If it is not revealed, how will a woman know you truly love her? And vice versa. Let me break it down. What is the definition of love? The definition of love is an intense feeling of affection. Feeling a deep romantic or sexual attachment to. When you have these strong feelings for the opposite sex it is up to you to exhibit your feelings with actions. I don't mean just by sex. Sex only satisfies the body. What about the mind and her heart? Displaying your signs of affection is the confirmation.

Women love to be catered by their men and vice versa. Breakfast in bed, unexpected romantic getaways, and sweet loving words to make her feel special like a queen. Whether it is a trip away from the monotony or a picnic at the park or scenic beach quality time is important in a relationship. Send beautiful sentiments such as cards and flowers to let her know you are thinking about her.

Body massages are a great way to relax her exhausted mind and body. It is not always about showering a woman with expensive gifts, but rather putting some thought into the moments to make it memorable.

Some men often complain about what they are not getting from the relationship too. I guarantee you if you exemplify this you will be catered by your woman. With delicious meals, love, and all the sex your body can stand. God created a woman for a man to cherish and respect. The woman will do the same in reciprocation. Do not try to run games and disrespect her. Treat a woman like you would treat your mother or sister. Hopefully, with the utmost honor, and respect. Women it is up to you to know the difference between love and abuse.

And to be able to decipher from the lies!

Selfishness in a loving relationship can only sabotage the love. When an individual is selfish, and only cares about themselves. It makes their partner feel neglected or alone. This can cause a person to become withdrawn, and lose their feelings altogether. It is always up to both people in a marriage or relationship to always be there for one another. No matter what the circumstances are! Never act as if you are too busy for your wife/girlfriend or husband/boyfriend. Because if you display this kind of behavior it can again cause your partner to stray away, and become withdrawn from you. Being in a marriage for a long amount of time does not guarantee he or she will NOT fall prey to infidelity. Because if he or she is looking for excitement they may want to feel like they're living again. It could easily happen. When you are truly in love it is what guarantees being faithful.

Sometimes, we can get too comfortable in our relationships or marriages.

Being too cozy in a relationship, and we start slipping. Something we can't do is get too comfortable. For example, letting our appearance go away, if we can help it. We have to always keep our appearance together. Always keep the sparks, and chemistry flowing. Especially in the bedroom. I don't consider myself to be an expert in the love department, but I have experienced a few situations in life, and my advice is solemnly based on my own experiences. I can tell you the worst feeling in the world is to feel totally alone in a marriage or any relationship!

# Who is to Blame...
## When love is just not there anymore?

Infidelity sucks! Especially when it happens to you. Honestly, I believe the majority of people cheat for a reason. What are the reasons? I am sure there is a percentage of people who cheat just for the heck of it. After doing my research, most women cheat for seven reasons. I am sure this applies to men as well. Here are the seven reasons:

1. Lack of Intimacy.
2. Lack of Communication
3. Hypersexuality
4. They Want to Check Out of the Relationship
5. You've Both Grown Apart
6. To Get Revenge
7. Immaturity

Infidelity Statistics are as follow. According to an article by James Smith that was published in July of 2018. In most all cases, men cheat more than women. In over 1/3 of marriages, one or more partners admit to cheating. 22% of men say that they've cheated on their significant other. 14% of women admit to cheating on their significant other. 36% of men and women admit to having an affair with a co-worker. 17% of men and women admit to having an affair with a sister-in-law or brother-in-law. People who have cheated before are 350% more likely cheat again. Affairs are most likely to occur two years into a marriage. 35% of men and women admit to cheating while on a business trip. 9%

of men admit they might have an affair to get back at a spouse. While everyone has their own reason for cheating there are common reasons why the majority of people do.

The minute we fall in love with an amazing person. We hope and pray their feelings are mutual. And the love will continue to last for an eternity. After days, develop into years of loving them unconditionally what happens when love changes and disappears? Who's to blame when love just isn't there anymore?

This chapter is going to get deeper than the abyss. My observations are based on the opinions of married couples. I have always been very analytical. Let us analyze and examine the question. The color red symbolizes passion. In order, to keep the flames going in a relationship or a marriage two people have to always keep it hot and spice it up. Otherwise the love will disintegrate, turning into dry ashes. When this occurs, it can be for many reasons. One being, overtime we can get too comfortable with our mates. We stop doing the nice special things that made us fall in love in the first place.

For example, showing some kind of gestures like writing cute love letters or whatever to express how much you care and love them. Becoming more of a homebody, instead of wanting to spend nights out on the town together. Of course, as we age our bodies slow down. It is factual, but just because you have slowed down does not mean your partner has slowed down too. Keep in mind of that! Because if not this is when it can become very boring. Love and marriage can be a lot of work. It is continuous and it never stops. Laziness is never acceptable. What you do not put into your relationship or marriage is exactly what you will get out of it... NOTHING!!!

Two people can simply grow apart from each other. Have you ever heard the saying the marriage has run its course? It can happen. Usually one person has out grown, and onto a whole another level. While the other is growing at a slower place or if they are growing at all, causing them to be unable to relate anymore.

The pressures of life can also be a contributing factor. Life is tough! It can be so stressful and overwhelming. It can cause a person to become withdrawn from the world and their mate too. Just mentally shut down.

Communication is key to any successful relationship or marriage. When you are feeling alone or no longer happy, it is up to you to inform your spouse. Instead of resorting to social media, to look for what you feel you are not getting at home.

Reframe from keeping secrets, because secrets only develop into pain. Pain turns into tears for the both of you. When the trust is broken, it is completely gone. No matter what, unfortunately it is difficult to get it back! After questioning several married couples, I come to the conclusion both people are responsible when love dies. There is no pointing the finger at who is at fault. Here is why? It goes right back to the communication factor. If the sex is no longer good anymore, it is up to you to discuss it with your partner. Always speak your mind. Whatever the problems are that is causing conflicts within your relationship or marriage say it.

The writing can be right there on the wall for you to see and do not ignore it. If you recognize the signs, confront your spouse. Before they confront you for a divorce!

People get married for all sorts of reasons. Love, sex, companionship, stability, and business. The list goes on and on. When I was younger and naïve, I always thought people got married for one reason and it was because of love. But that is not always the case or true. I guess I was living in a fairytale kind of world. Some women and men may fall in love at first sight. But for some, love does not come automatic. It takes time to blossom like a plant. Love has to be watered and nurtured, so it can blossom and develop into something beautiful.

Let's talk about sex. I bet those eyes got really big. It is most people's favorite topic to talk about. Yeah... SEX. A lot of people confuse love and sex. My definition and perception of love is... Love satisfies the heart and stimulates the mind. While sex recharges only the body. One is no good without the other. It is healthy when the chemistry is strong. The feelings are intensified and mutual. It is beautiful when that special someone consumes your thoughts and dreams. He or she makes you feel totally alive. Is sex necessary for a happy marriage? Depending on the couple, the two must have an understanding of their expectations of each other.

Sex does play an important role, in any relationship or marriage. But it should not be based on it. A metaphysical relationship is the best form of love. Because once the mind is satisfied, the body is too. Intensified emotions are built up over time. Metaphysically bringing on an intense feeling, which makes having sex even more pleasurable and gratifying. Instead of vice versa. Sex without love never last, but it can work for some people. It depends on the kind of relationship you desire.

Like the old saying, "whatever floats your boat!"


Follow Yetta Yvette on Goodreads, Facebook, Instagram, and Twitter.
Call the National Domestic Abuse Hotline and say no to abuse 1-800-799-SAFE (7233)

# Yetta's Prayer

Thank You God for this beautiful day your guidance and favor. I pray for anyone who is in great pain with the recent loss of a loved one. Lord, heal their heart and comfort their soul. For only time can heal the woe.

In your Son's Jesus Name,
Amen

# WAXING POETIC

# Say a Prayer

Say a prayer when in doubt.
Say a prayer when you feel you are without.
Say a prayer when you feel all alone.
Say a prayer when your love ones leave this earth and now
have gone on.
Say a prayer when people are cruel to you for no apparent
reason.
Always remember you can say a prayer no matter what the
season.

# Ocean

When I look out into the ocean,
I am mesmerized.
It gives me clarity to my mind and hardens my inner soul.
One of God's most lovely creations.
Sensations are flowing all through my flesh.
Whenever I am being tested by the world,
all I have to do is glance out into the ocean.
The waves are swarming.
The sound is amazing, the air is so crisp,
and not to mention the smell salty.
It rewinds me back into an unlocked state of mind.
I am in a time when life can become so cruel to you.
As the years pass, it seems to only get tougher and tougher.
But you gotta hang tight...
Storms don't last for eternity and eventually,
the sun rays will shine on you so bright!

# I wonder Y?

*Part 1*
Conversations with Myself

O, Lord I feel the pain.
It makes me want to go insane.
I know there will be better days ahead.
Trust in you, that is exactly what I am intending to do.
A tear drops from my eye and I wonder Y?
Y is the world the way that it is?
Some may say we are living in our last days.
And some will say it is just the sign of the times.
Like daddy always used to say, only the strong survive in
this jungle.
Through God's grace that has definitely proven to be me.
Just as strong as a Leo Lion's roar and as tough as the skin
on a wild boar.
I am strong as I can be.
I keep my armor on and fight.
I can finally see my light in the dark tunnel of this life!
I work hard every day and block out what the negative
people (HATERS) have to say.
And before you know it, I will be on my way.

# Girl Bye!
## *In the words of Karter Stephens*

I miss the woman, I fell in love with years ago.
The one who would not lie nor cheat.
Do you remember her?
The one who would not be so insensitive and cruel to me.
The one who would not want to cut me so deep.
I loved a woman who was so sweet.
The one who brought me back to life and sweep me off my feet.
The woman who made me strong when things went wrong in my life.
The woman who made me want to live, instead of die.
I pray she comes back to me and if not, I guess I will have to say girl bye!

# When a Heart Breaks

When a heart breaks, it shatters to the ground.
Without making a sound.
And love is now lost and it can't be found.
How can you repair it again?
You gotta start all over and be ready to mend.
Are you ready to work for the love you lost, my friend?
Just realize that there is going to be an expensive cost.
Because the heart is fragile and torn apart.
You will have to put the pieces back together from the start.
Piece by piece like a puzzle.
Show signs of affection like nuzzle.
You have to make the other person realize that you truly
messed up.
Take the blame and it is time to confess up.
Don't ever take love and a person for granted.
Because who you don't love, someone else will on the
planet.

# I Wonder Y
*Part 2*

My brain sparks
When I sit here and look to the moon
It's full, just like my thoughts
I have always had a wandering mind
It never stops!
When I was younger, it did the same
I couldn't figure it out
I was a little bit different
I analyze the world and it's insane
I would ask, "Why this and that?"
And I still don't know
You can't let it wreck your brain
But what I do know
It's gonna be a beautiful night

# If I Were a Man

I would truly understand
How to treat a woman
Beautiful
Soft like fur
A queen
To be respected
And to never be disrespected or neglected
The tears she cries
Because of the lies
But why?
When there is beauty by your side
Step up and be the King
The ultimate goal is a love thing
God chose you
To do her right
Instead of arguments in the late night
How about touch of caress
Echoes of I love you
Ending up in I dos
Cards, flowers, and candy for no apparent reason at all
That's love
It's your call
There's always a choice
You don't have to
But man, you got to understand
When you don't do this
You can lose a woman!

# Q & A with Yetta Yvette

*What inspired you to write Age Ain't Nothing but a Number, and Football Superstar?*

I had a calling. God placed it on my heart. I know someone in this crazy world is dealing with the exact stories at hand. I wanted to share my story, so I can enlighten anyone who is caught up in a similar situation. Hopefully, for happier results. We are actresses, and actors in our own movies. Some of us are in dramas, comedies, and maybe even horrors. We go through similar situations in life. I love to write amazing stories, on people who are tested and even challenged. We get knocked down, but you have to get up and keep on pushing! People who are relentless, tenacious, and overcome certain obstacles is what inspires me to write great stories.

*Who are some of your favorite authors?*

My favorite Dr. Maya Angelou. I love truth, in a story. Non-Fiction authors have my heart, because I feel those are the hardest stories to write.

*What is the best thing about being a creative writer?*

I love expressing my thoughts on paper. I feel totally free! My stories are designed to enlighten, inspire, and motivate YOU! If I can make you feel the emotions, I have done my job.

### When is your favorite time to write?

I come alive in the night time. When I am creating a story, I love to write late/early mornings. I am talking, like 1a.m. When it is extremely quiet, and collectively is when I am most creative, and the juices are flowing. Once I have the story altogether, I will do my plugins and edits in the day.

### What was your favorite subject in school?

C'mon, hands down English. Although, I did not take writing seriously, until later in college. Thank you to my many English teachers.

### How do you deal with writer's block?

I write about true life, so there is always a topic to discuss. I am strong in my faith, so I pray to God and ask. I am just the messenger. God puts it on my heart, and I will write it. If I get stuck with writer's block, I will take a break from my story. Normally, my thoughts hit me throughout the day. So, I have to keep a pen, and pad on standby.

### What's your advice for aspiring writers?

First, you have to love what you do, in order to be successful at it. It has to be your number one passion. Stay true to yourself and always practice your craft!
Stay creative =)

### What are you currently working on?

I love writing based on/inspired by true stories when people are extremely challenged and overcome their obstacles. I was flabbergasted when my nieces and nephew told me they were interested in writing a children's book. LOL. Actually, I thought it was cute! My response, "Are you sure you guys can pull it off?" "Can you write?" They said, "Yes!" And I will agree. These kiddos hit you with their first sentences to captivate your interest. I am so proud of you Lyric, Jaelyn, and Devin. They persuaded me to write a children's book and of course, with their assistance. It is now in production! The Children's Story coming soon!

When it drops, be sure to check it out!

### How do you get inspired to write?

Certain locations will make me get deep into my thoughts than others and it is when I am really creative and the juices are flowing. I like different locations like the beach, or a park. A nice quiet tranquil place, with some music is a plus and especially Prince's music. It always puts me in a good mood to write.

### What are your pet peeves?

I really don't like to complain, because it is not my style. But what disappoints me is when I hear people say they don't need love. Everybody needs love! It is such a beautiful thing! Contrary to what most people may believe, love is what makes the world go around! Another pet peeve of mine is when people are cruel just to be cruel to you. Do you know how to get revenge on people who don't like you for no apparent reason? Kill them with kindness. Sometimes it is tough, but it works every time. Lastly, one more thing that aggravates me is a lie, so live in your truth! Nothing gets me more fueled, than a person who will quote the Bible whenever it is convenient for them to do so. I mean up and down...all day every day and then when they're faced with life's situation towards mankind, you don't see the so-called Christian in them anymore, at all. Now it is truly amazing to me and not to mention questionable, too. If you are going to quote the Bible 24/7 it's all good! But LIVE by it 24/7. WE MUST STRIVE TO QUOTE AND LIVE EVERYDAY BY IT!

### What fuels your thoughts?

Pain and a world of sin. There is so much calamity going on in the world today, it always seems to give me plenty of material to write about. LOL God's voice will tug away at my heart. I pay very close attention and I will decide to write freely, whatever is on my mind.

www.ingramcontent.com/pod-product-compliance
Lightning Source LLC
Chambersburg PA
CBHW050728030426
42336CB00012B/1456